Hunting Wild Turkeys
with Ray Eye

Hunting Wild Turkeys with Ray Eye

Michael Pearce
and
Ray Eye

Stackpole Books

Copyright © 1990 by Stackpole Books

Published by
STACKPOLE BOOKS
Cameron and Kelker Streets
P.O. Box 1831
Harrisburg, PA 17105

All rights reserved, including the right to reproduce this book or portions thereof in any form or by any means, electronic or mechanical, including photocopying, recording, or by any information storage and retrieval system, without permission in writing from the publisher. All inquiries should be addressed to Stackpole Books, Cameron and Kelker Streets, P.O. Box 1831, Harrisburg, Pennsylvania 17105.

Printed in the United States of America

10 9 8 7 6 5 4 3 2 1

First Edition

Cover photograph by Greg Murphy (a Ray Eye Enterprises photo)
Jacket design by Tracy Patterson

Library of Congress Cataloging-in-Publication Data

Pearce, Michael, 1958–
    Hunting wild turkeys with Ray Eye / Michael Pearce and Ray Eye. — 1st ed.
      p. cm.
    ISBN 0-8117-0866-7 : $22.95
    1. Turkey hunting. I. Eye, Ray, 1952– . II. Title.
SK325.T8P43   1990
799.2′48619—dc20
                                                  89-37624
                                                     CIP

This book is dedicated to the wild turkey.

We also dedicate this book to the landowners, turkey hunters, conservation organizations, and game commissions whose combined efforts made possible the restoration and the current management of the wild turkey. Without their support, this book and turkey hunting as we now know it would not be possible.

Acknowledgments

It would be impossible to thank everyone who has, in one way or another, assisted in the completion of this book. It has taken years of planning, writing, and photography to make this project a reality.

Special gratitude is expressed to Gerry Bethge, Debbie Bender, John Blumb, Ken Cook, Kathy Czapla, Buford and Melissa Eye, Joe and Clemy Eye, Janet Eye, Marty Eye, Terry Funk, H. D. Harrison, John Hauer, Arlon Held, Ben "Bear" Held, Mike and Belinka Held, Tom Huggler, Bubba Jones, Dale Kuen, Pat Leonard, Greg Murphy, Kathy Pearce, Milton Rose, Scott Schaefer, Mike Smyth, Vince Thompson, Verle Pemberton and Denny Dennis.

Most importantly, we'd like to thank our families for their support, remarkable patience, and understanding.

Contents

	Foreword by Gerry Bethge	13
	Introduction	17
1	**The Beginning** *My First Hunt*	19
2	**Turkeys** *Distribution and life cycle*	25
3	**Turkey Talk** *Calls turkeys make, what they mean*	41
4	**Talking Turkey** *How hunters communicate with turkeys*	47
5	**Calling Devices** *Various kinds of calls, how to use them*	53
6	**Scouting** *Preseason looking and listening*	69

7	Spring Hunting	79
	Basics for the most popular season	
8	Roosting	81
	Finding a roosted turkey in the evening	
9	Duel at Dawn	85
	Calling and working a roosted bird	
10	After Flydown	91
	Finding and calling on the ground	
11	Calling Positions	95
	Setting up to call a bird	
12	Strutting Areas	103
	Finding and hunting strutting areas	
13	Gobblers with Hens	111
	Handling a bird that's already taken	
14	Late Spring	117
	Hunting during premating season	
15	Birds in Bad Weather	119
	Handling wind, rain, and snow	
16	Hunting Pressure	125
	Outsmarting birds accustomed to hunters	
17	Hangups	129
	Toms that gobble but won't come in	
18	Blind Calling	133
	Moving and calling to silent toms	
19	The Buddy System	137
	Teaming up for success	
20	The Harvest	141
	Taking the turkey	

21	**Fall Hunting** *Tactics for autumn*	**147**
22	**Bowhunting** *How to succeed with bow and arrow*	**159**
23	**Equipment** *Guns, Bows, Boots, etc.*	**169**
24	**Safety** *How to hunt safely*	**191**
25	**Turkeys I've Known** *My favorite turkey personalities*	**195**
26	**Turkey Tales**	**201**
27	**The Future**	**207**

Foreword

Ray Eye was the last grown man I hugged — there, I said it. Now, stop laughing because it wasn't anything like that. This story begins back in 1984 when *Outdoor Life*'s Kansas editor Mike Pearce dragged me to Missouri for a spring turkey hunt. I guess "dragged" really isn't the most accurate term, since I kind of invited myself on the hunt, but my family may be reading this and they're still under the impression that I have to hunt turkeys because it's part of my job as an outdoor magazine editor. Suffice it to say that I was ruined after hearing my very first gobble — and they say drug addiction is bad.

Through no fault of Ray's, I didn't get a bird on that hunt. Rude hunters (although I think Ray called them something else) messed up at least a half dozen opportunities; and I messed up at least once.

I wasn't disappointed, though, because I had a plan. The plan was to get this hotshot turkey hunter on my turf in Massachusetts the next year and see what he could do. My reasoning was actually more sentimental than it sounds: I wanted to take my very first gobbler in woods that, through the years, had almost become my second home.

The gobbler we roosted the night before opening day clung to a tree limb just ten short walking minutes from my Berkshire home. It was a walk that seemed to take hours, though, as we headed in under the predawn skies.

"Slow down," Ray kept whispering. "We got plenty of time."

"But it's starting to get light already," I answered back. His nonchalance was infuriating, especially since I knew he was right.

As we crested the ridge, Ray halted me and belted out an owl hoot that seemed way too loud to me. I mean, there aren't even any barred owls in Massachusetts. Wrong again. Just a tad early to wake up the roosted tom but not too soon to call in a couple of laughing barred owls.

"Stay here, I'll be right back," Ray whispered.

"Wha. . . . where you going?" I frantically replied. "Oh man, c'mon, we gotta set up on that bird."

"Plenty of time," was all he said. I wanted to kill him.

"Loosen up, guy," he said upon his return. "We got a turkey to shoot."

With that he hooted again. That tom was right where we had left him the night before, gobbling just as loud as he could. I winced with every step I took in the crunchy leaves as Ray pointed out my set-up location. "Get your gun up and stay ready," were his departing words.

Ready — I'd been ready a couple of hours ago. Nonetheless, I took his advice and waited for Ray to do his magic. And what magic it was. Soft tree yelps were the first sweet words spoken to the gobbler that morning, seemingly driving the bird insane. It was barely shooting light when I heard him fly down. Now Ray got aggressive and that old bird just kept gobbling and closing ground. Then a hitch in the program. Ray was set up about thirty-five yards behind me and just a bit to my left. Guess where the bird went?

I was dying inside. Would I ever get a shot? But Ray wasn't done yet. Just as I adjusted my shotgun to a severe 45 degree angle, he adjusted his calling. With the prowess of Edgar Bergen, he threw his voice to the right and turned that bird on a dime. I could hear the gobbler drumming now and knew that the moment of truth was about to arrive. Then I saw the bird . . . and the beard. A blowdown lay between us, and with just a one foot gap to shoot through, I put the bead on its head, put my cheek to the stock and pulled the trigger.

We arrived at the same time: about a millisecond after the shot. That gobbler was about the prettiest sight I've ever seen. There was blood everywhere — mine.

"Gawd, are you okay?" Ray said. "Your nose is a mess."

I wasn't feeling any pain, but I had apparently kept my face on that stock too well, because I had a severe nosebleed.

That's when I hugged him. Hey, it seemed like the thing to do at the time. We looked the bird over for several minutes as hunters are wont to do and retold the events that had just transpired two or three times.

"Let's go get some breakfast," I suggested to Ray.

"Nah," he said. "You need to sling that bird over your shoulder and walk out of here on your own, buddy."

He was right again. I had walked that same tote road a thousand times over the years, but it never appeared as beautiful as it did that morning. I stopped four or five times along the way—to rest, I told myself—but I know differently now. When I came to the lake at the end of the road, the sun was just coming up above the treeline. A flight of geese and a pair of wood ducks flew over as I just lay there atop the grass-covered dam and enjoyed the morning, looking at my gobbler.

I wasn't home more than a half hour when Ray came trudging into the house.

"Get a bird?" I asked, more because that's what turkey hunters ask each other than because I actually thought he had gotten one.

"Yeh," he said. There was that nonchalance again.

"Bull," I replied. "How'd you have enough time? I just left you."

Well, he did get a nice longbeard, and then proceeded to call in another the next morning for my buddy Ralph Stuart. Three longbeards in two days. Quite a hunt; quite a hunter.

Ray Eye and Mike Pearce—I blame them entirely for an affliction I have yet to recover from. To be honest, I hope I never do.

Gerry Bethge
Senior Editor, *Outdoor Life*

Introduction

A few years ago at a Kansas City Seminar, a young hunter, probably no more than fourteen or fifteen, battled his way through a circle of people to where I was standing and nervously asked me, "Mr. Eye, what is THE most important part of turkey hunting . . . what's THE thing that separates the experts from the rest?"

Not a year goes by that I don't get asked a similar question at least a dozen times. Turkey hunters across the nation are looking for that one solution to all their problems. If you are one of those, I'm afraid you're going to be disappointed in this book, because it doesn't contain THE answer.

That's because there is no one secret for success. To do consistently well at turkey hunting takes a combination of skills, all of which are important. A lot of people worry so much about calling that they forget such things as knowing the birds, being familiar with their hunting territory, having the right equipment, and realizing their own capabilities.

There are some things that simply can't be learned from a book — in the end, the best teacher is always experience. I've been at this game for over a quarter of a century and I'm still learning something new and important every year.

But the odds are more in your favor than ever before. Our country is virtually being overrun with turkeys. Each year more and more states are reporting record harvests as the flocks continue to increase.

Today's equipment is a great deal better than it was even a decade ago. And turkey hunters have a wealth of information within their reach. When I started, the only way to learn was from the birds. Now hunters can attend seminars and calling contests, watch videos, and read magazine articles and, of course, books such as this one.

Remember, simply reading this book won't turn a novice into an expert overnight. What it can do, however, is save a lot of time getting from one stage to the other by learning from my years of mistakes and successes.

1
The Beginning

My grandfather took one last sip of coffee, pushed his breakfast plate aside, and stood as he pulled out his pocketwatch. Opening the lid on the old timepiece, he said, "You'd better be going, boy, if you want to kill a turkey."

His words caught me off guard, so much so that it was several seconds before I could stammer a reply. "But Pop, aren't you going with me . . . ? I've never been turkey hunting before."

"I'd like to, Ray, but you know I've got chores to do," he answered, putting a hand on my shoulder. "Besides, the only way you're really going to learn is to get up there and do it by yourself. Now come on, you'd better get going."

I stood there in a state of shock and watched the old man leave the room to get his trusted Winchester 97 and a handful of shells. Following him to the back door, I still couldn't believe what was happening.

Just outside the door he reached up and took down a kerosene lantern, scratched a match against its base, lit it, and handed it to me. "You know where to go on the mountain and what to do, boy. God knows we've been through it enough," he said as he stuffed the shotgun shells into my faded bib overalls. "Just remember what I've told you and be careful." He placed the shotgun in my other hand and gave me a pat on the back that nudged me on my way.

Holding the lantern high I headed across the yard, now more scared than excited. Those first few steps that I took as a nine-year-old were the toughest I'd ever taken — or would ever take.

Some of my first memories are of the weekends spent on my grandparents' farm deep in the Missouri Ozarks. Located three miles up a valley, or "holler" as they call it in the hills, the farm had been the home of three generations in my family.

The white, two-story farmhouse was typical for the hills. A clear, spring-fed creek ran only a few yards from the front door, past the barn and other outbuildings. The house sat in a rare Ozark meadow, surrounded on three sides by steep evergreen- and hardwood-covered hills. The highest of the hills was simply referred to as "the mountain," because it was one of the highest points in the state.

In 1962, the year I headed up the mountain that dark morning, most of America was in the middle of a rapid modernization. Not so in the backcountry around the farm. Life had changed little since my dad was born in the house decades before.

Electricity had just arrived, but indoor plumbing hadn't and the telephone never did. The roads were a far cry from what most Americans were used to. During the spring, the dirt path leading to Grandpa's turned into a muddy trough.

But there were advantages to living such a life. For one thing, it was simple. Everything was hard work and you did the best you could with what was at hand. Also, there was a closeness between family and friends that sometimes slips away with progress.

The primitivism of the mountains made them sanctuaries for wildlife. Small game was abundant, and deer and turkeys had never been pushed or shot out of the rough backcountry. Hunting was a way of life, as much a means of putting food on the table as it was recreation. Like previous generations, I was educated at an early age. I listened to men tell old hunting tales and tagged along on squirrel hunts before I was five.

I loved it all, but turkeys held a particular fascination. They seemed to possess an almost mystical quality. They were rarely seen but always there. I can remember one spring morning like yesterday. Black storm clouds were marching over the mountain, and Pop and I were hurrying to get the last of the chores done.

With the first rumble of thunder came a gobble from a nearby ridge, then another and another. I stood there, my mouth hanging open in amazement as the hills around the farm came alive with gobbles. Pop finally snapped me out of my trance and we made it to the house just as the first of the big raindrops banged down on the tin roof.

The Beginning

As a youngster, I had turkeys on my mind constantly. In the woods I was always looking for turkeys and I always asked my dad to explain any kind of evidence of their presence. I badgered poor Grandpa relentlessly, asking him to retell stories about turkey hunting when he was young. Looking back, I now realize he showed a great deal of patience and answered most questions to my satisfaction. Except for one: "When will I be old enough to hunt turkeys?" "Someday" was his standard answer.

One fall day his answer changed. The smell of homemade bread was in the air as we cut wood for the cookstove. Pausing to watch me work, Pop smiled and said out of the blue, "Ray, I think you'll be big enough by next spring." He didn't need to explain; I knew exactly what he meant.

A little later he gave me what became my most prized possession—my own turkey call. Grandpa had made it by hand, using a piece of slate from the chalkboard at an old one-room schoolhouse. For a striker he'd cut a piece of cedar from a fencepost and fit it in the bottom of a hollowed-out corncob.

The call was my life and I practiced religiously. Teachers took the call away from me more than once for using it at school. Grandma said I sounded like "a cat caught in a fence" and Pop kept telling me to keep practicing.

The winter of 1961-62 was the longest of my life, but it eventually ended. Turkey season was only a week away when Pop shook me awake one cold April morning and said, "Get up. We're going up on the mountain for a while."

I did my best to keep up with him in the predawn darkness as we crossed the creek, headed across the dew-covered pasture, and found the old trail that would take us up the mountain. We walked quietly until we came to a huge oak at the junction of two ridges.

I started to ask one of the dozens of questions that were floating in my mind but Grandpa quickly silenced me with a finger to his lips. Cupping his hands around his mouth, he let loose an imitation of a barred owl. Imagine how I felt when a turkey gobbled down the ridge to the northwest.

We stood there for a while and listened to the sounds of turkeys gobbling all over the hills. Each time one called, the bird in front of us rifled back a reply.

As we turned to leave, Pop whispered, "This is the place, boy. You'll want to sit with your back against that big oak, facing down that ridge. Use your call and whatever you do don't move until you're ready to come home."

I was a bundle of nerves and anticipation the night before my hunt.

Hoping to make the next day arrive faster, I slipped into bed after supper, already wearing my hunting clothes, except for my oversized work jacket and old tennis shoes.

Sleep was slow to come. I lay in bed listening to the calls of the whippoorwills, the coyotes yipping on the mountain, and the steady sound of the stream flowing nearby. I'd been awake for hours when the smell of homemade biscuits and frying bacon and eggs drifted upstairs.

Normally I'd have devoured the breakfast in front of me in a matter of minutes, but not that morning. I picked at the meal and never took my eyes off Grandpa.

When he broke the news that I'd be hunting alone I was heartbroken. For years I'd pictured us hunting together. The thought of trying for one of the mountain's phantom birds alone was beyond my young imagination.

I tried to present myself as a man as I headed toward the creek. In some ways today brought the realization of a lifelong dream. I was going up on the mountain to try to kill a turkey. The fact that I was carrying Grandpa's favorite shotgun was an accomplishment. But inside I was as scared as I'd ever been.

My hands full, I had trouble crossing the stream. Midway across I missed a steppingstone and ended up knee-deep in cold water. I made my way across the pasture, wet shoes squeaking with every step.

I'd walked the trail to the top of the mountain dozens of times, but never had it seemed so long or so frightening. I finally arrived at the big oak, put out the lantern, and sat down.

I strained to remember everything Grandpa had told me as I quietly slipped the blue paper shells into the pumpgun. I sat there shivering from both cold and fear, desperately hoping Pop would come walking up the trail.

With the reddening of the eastern horizon came the sounds of life in the timber. At first I heard only songbirds, and I began to relax a little. Then came the eight-note call of a barred owl. I caught my breath when the turkey gobbled from down the ridge.

I picked up the slate call but couldn't use it. I was afraid, afraid I'd goof up and scare the turkey and ruin my dream. Again and again I tried to rub the cedar against the slate but each time I pulled back. Finally I shut my eyes, swallowed the huge lump in my throat and shakingly rubbed the peg against the call. I winced at the gosh-awful noise it produced.

Whether it was in response to my call or just coincidence I'll never know, but the gobbler sounded off. Several more times I tried to force some yelps from the call but couldn't. I finally dropped the call in frustration and clutched the gun that was resting on my knees.

By then I could hear turkeys gobbling all around me, the closest two being the bird in front of me and a tom on the next ridge. I waited and listened to the birds gobbling; I could tell they were not moving.

Suddenly came the soft yelps of a hen turkey behind me. I began to panic, fearing the hen would call the gobblers away from me. I started to get up to move closer to the hen but suddenly I remembered Pop saying, "Whatever you do, don't move. . . ." Even though it looked hopeless I stayed.

Soon the three birds were calling almost nonstop and the two gobblers were headed my way. Then I realized that the hen was actually a blessing. To get to her the gobblers would have to walk right past me. Since I was too nervous to call she was my only hope.

I could hear the two toms getting closer to each other but wasn't prepared for what came next. From just below the ridge came the loud noises of deep turkey purrs, flapping wings, and feathered bodies thumping together.

I didn't know it at the time, but the two birds were fighting for the hen. I was shaking so hard I thought for sure the turkeys would see me, and the end of the gun barrel was drawing circles the size of donuts.

Hearing the sounds of tree limbs breaking I watched a big turkey rise through the trees and sail out across the valley. A loud, triumphant gobble sounded from the scene of the battle, and the hen responded with a series of clucks and yelps. My pounding heart went into overdrive. Breathing was hard and my black-rimmed glasses started to fog.

The next time the tom sounded off he was so close I could hear a rattle in his gobble. Like a ghost he suddenly appeared to my right, head tucked back, feathers puffed out and wings dragging the ground.

My first response was to swing the gun and shoot, but in the back of mind I heard Pop stressing, "Never move a muscle when you can see the turkey's head. If you do he'll spot you for sure. And remember to aim just for the head."

Seconds seemed like hours but I waited. When the bird stepped behind a big hickory I twisted my body, cocked the hammer, and raised the gun. There was a deafening boom as the old gun went off when the turkey stepped back into view. In my haste I'd tucked the stock under my arm and the old Winchester had raised up and struck me in the face, bloodying my nose and sending my glasses flying.

Holding onto the gun with one hand I rummaged through the leaves, found my broken glasses, and poked them on my face as I ran to where

I'd last seen the bird. My foot caught a root and I tumbled down the ridge. When I finally stopped rolling I looked up and there he was, stretched out, his feathers glistening in the sun.

I arrived down at the farm, soaking wet, covered with mud and blood, half dragging and half carrying a turkey that weighed half as much as I did. Grandpa heard my shouts and was waiting for me.

He admired the bird, congratulated me and then laughingly said, "You'd better run along and get yourself cleaned up before your grandma has a fit." I spent the rest of the day telling and re-telling him how I'd killed the big gobbler, fibbing a little by explaining how I'd called the bird myself. He smiled and listened to every word.

A lot's changed since then. My life has never been the same. After I took that turkey, I was in the woods calling every spare minute I had. It cost me girlfriends, it cost me jobs, and it almost got me kicked out of school several times. But it was an addiction I wouldn't have cured if I could have.

I learned a lot about calling turkeys that April morning and I've learned a lot since. In fact I've learned enough to make my living at it. I started my own successful company, Ray Eye Enterprises, giving seminars throughout the country; I've guided for over fifteen years and have won major calling contests nationwide.

Grandpa and Grandma had to move off the farm and into a small community nearby. Grandma's still there and still teases me about sounding like "a cat caught in a fence." Grandpa died in 1976.

It wasn't long after his death that the entire family was gathered at Grandma's. As usual, the talk turned to hunting and someone brought up the subject of my first turkey. My eyes began to moisten and I walked over and leaned against the fence to look out towards the mountain that held so many fond memories of Pop.

A few seconds later I felt Grandma's hand softly rub my shoulder as she said, "You're thinking of Pop, aren't you?" Never taking my eyes off the mountain I bit my lip and nodded my head.

She lovingly moved in beside me and softly said, "Ray, do you remember that hen on the mountain the morning you killed your first turkey?"

I looked at her, swallowed hard and said, "Yes."

"That wasn't a hen calling behind you," she said, "that was your grandpa."

2
Turkeys

I suppose it is possible for a turkey hunter to spend his entire gobbler-chasing career knowing only what it takes to kill the birds within his hunting grounds. But his ignorance of the turkey's biology would deprive him of a chance to add even greater satisfaction to his sport.

Knowing the history and biology of *Meleagris gallopavo* gives a hunter an added respect and admiration for what many call the greatest game species in America.

No one knows for sure how long the gobble of the wild turkey has echoed across what is now called America. Archeological digs have shown that native Americans used turkeys for a variety of reasons thousands of years before the first European explorer saw his first turkey.

Turkeys thrived for centuries, occupying a range that covered roughly the eastern half of the country as well as much of the Southwest. Some have estimated that the population may have reached eight to ten million.

The earliest settlers found the birds not only abundant, but easily harvested and popular on the table. Unfortunately they were a little too popular. By the early part of the twentieth century, loss of habitat, baiting, roost-shooting, and other means of slaughtering turkeys had significantly reduced their numbers.

An adult gobbler's head and neck. Compared to the hen, the gobbler is usually larger in size and has more coloration of red, white, and blue. But the best identification is always to look for a visible beard. *Photo by Ray Eye.*

A hen turkey's head. A hen is always smaller in size and lighter in color, and has feathers that run all the way to the crest of her head. *Photo by Ray Eye.*

The gobble of the wild turkey was largely limited to a few scattered pockets of wilderness. Some predicted that the birds would follow the path of the endangered buffalo, and possibly the extinct passenger pigeon.

But with the advent of modern game management the hope was for turkeys to not only survive but to possibly recapture some of their original range. But the turkeys' comeback has no doubt surpassed the wildest dreams of those who first trapped and transplanted turkeys in the 1940s and 1950s.

The springtime calls of gobblers and hens can now be heard in every state except Alaska. Turkeys are thriving in states where they were historically absent.

State game departments deserve much of the credit, as do conservation organizations like the National Wild Turkey Federation. Yet the birds themselves deserve most of the credit. Given a chance, wild turkeys waste little time taking a foothold.

Wild turkey hens have a natural ability to pull off huge clutches and hatches to fill under-utilized habitat. Releases of three toms and nine hens have grown to estimated flocks of hundreds of turkeys in as little as five years.

Flocks have also expanded to, and are thriving in, habitat that was thought to be unsuitable as recently as the early 1980s. As of early 1989, the potential of this remarkable gamebird to further expand its range is still unknown.

Wild turkeys probably inhabit as wide a range of habitat as any game bird in the United States, from the desert lowlands to the swamps of Florida and the pine-covered ridges of the Rocky Mountains.

Through the centuries turkeys learned to adapt to their environments, developing into several recognizable subspecies. The four most common in the United States are the eastern, Merriam, Rio Grande, and Florida, or Osceola.

Some hunters talk as if the four were almost distinct species. In truth they have far more in common than not. They all possess the eyes of an eagle, the ears of a white-tailed deer, and the paranoia of a coyote.

There is some debate about the ease of harvesting the various turkeys. Many eastern hunters have returned from prairie hunts with tales of quick success and "stupid" gobblers.

But it's my experience that the higher success rates on western turkeys have more to do with the amount of habitat, current conditions, and hunting pressure. Heavily hunted Rio Grandes have ignored my best calls and rattled my confidence during an unusually late spring. And farmland easterns that had never been hunted were nearly impossible to spook after they came to calls.

An adult hen feeding in a field. Proper identification is very important in turkey hunting to keep from shooting hens. *Photo by Ray Eye.*

The four subspecies are also more adaptable than commonly believed. Historically the Rio Grande was found throughout western Texas and up into southern Oklahoma. Now this bird is common as far north as Kansas and Nebraska. Believe it or not, explorer and naturalist accounts show that the eastern, known as the noble turkey of the hardwood forests, was the original turkey on the plains of Kansas and Oklahoma.

The four subspecies have enough in common that they interbreed. In fact interbreeding is often encouraged. Terry Funk, a Kansas turkey biologist, tells how the northwestern part of his state was once occupied by a stagnating flock of Rio Grandes. A few eastern toms were released in the land of mule deer and prairie dogs. The easterns not only survived, but helped create a virtual population explosion. Intentional stockings of eastern toms and Rio Grande hens have flourished in other places as well.

But no matter which bird you hunt, they all have a way of doubling your pulse and electrifying your nerves. They each possess their own special way of making even the most experienced hunter look like a rank amateur.

Turkeys

Eastern

The most populous and well-known of the four, eastern turkeys occupy a range from northern Florida to Maine, from the Atlantic seaboard to central Kansas. Often heavily hunted in a seemingly endless sea of habitat, easterns are possibly the most challenging of all turkeys.

Osceola

One of the toughest aspects of bagging Osceolas is simply getting a chance to hunt them. Found only in parts of Florida, Osceolas are far from pushovers. As with turkey hunting in other parts of the South, the swamps that these gobblers so love can make for challenging, and often very wet, hunting.

Merriam

The turkeys of the western United States, Merriams often come readily to calls, but a lack of understory in their habitat makes it difficult for the hunter to remain hidden long enough to bag this bird. To me these

Adult eastern gobbler. Note the visible beard protruding from the chest area, the larger overall size, and the more upright appearance that distinguish him from a hen. *Photo by Ray Eye.*

Close-up of an adult gobbler's beard. The beard is actually a primitive feather. Beard lengths vary according to habitat. Older birds often have longer beards, but beard length is not an accurate measure of a turkey's age. *Photo by Ray Eye.*

turkeys always sound farther away than they really are. There are good populations of this bird on public ground. The Black Hills of South Dakota itself offers close to a million acres of Merriam hunting. Scouting can be as important as it is with easterns.

Rio Grande

Often living in limited habitat, Rio Grandes in Texas, Oklahoma, and Kansas offer the highest success rates for hunters of the four subspecies. But the open terrain can work in favor of the sharp-eyed birds as well.

Sneaking into a calling sight can take some planning and effort. Hunters must be well concealed and must remain perfectly still.

Trophies

Interestingly enough, each of the four subspecies has its advantages over the others. The Osceolas, obviously, are the rarest and can have some impressive spurs. Easterns tend to be bigger in beard length and body size.

The ivory tips on back and tail feathers make the Merriams the most beautiful. The light coloring of the Rio Grandes makes them a close second to the Merriams in terms of looks. But my favorite characteristic of the dryland turkeys is their open habitat, which sometimes makes it possible to watch the bird work for hundreds of yards.

A Rio Grande in full strut. The white-tipped back and tail feathers make the Rio Grande one of the prettiest turkeys. *Photo by Mike Blair.*

One common denominator for comparing the quality of birds is spur length. Tag a bird that can be hung on a tree limb by his spurs and you've taken one of America's finest trophies, whether he's a sixteen-pound Texas Rio Grande or a twenty-six-pound Iowa eastern.

A Turkey's Life Cycle

For close to four weeks, the hen sits beneath the little tangle of briers. She had previously come for only a short while each day, depositing an egg or two onto the leaves, then departing.

Though there are no absolutes in wildlife, the hen probably laid an average clutch of twelve, and with the final egg her vigil began. The three-year-old hen could sit nearly motionless for hours, leaving her nest only to pick a few bugs or greens and to get a quick drink from the nearby stream.

And so far she has been lucky. A nest at the other end of the overgrown field had been discovered and demolished by a raccoon. Other nests in the area had been destroyed by farm machinery, or raided by skunks and a host of other animals.

This adult hen is in an old farm field close to water that she is using for a nesting area. Wild turkey hens build their nests on the ground and use brushy cover when available. *Photo by Ray Eye.*

The previous year her first clutch had met a similar fate. The old hen had been forced to re-nest and try again, with a smaller number of eggs.

On the twenty-eighth day of her wait the eggs begin to pop apart and the small, two-inch chicks step into the world. Soon ten of the dozen eggs had hatched. For a reason known only to nature, the other pair never would.

In a matter of hours the hen's life changes from one of peace to seeming pandemonium as she tries to oversee the young turkeys. The day-old poults can walk amazingly well as they follow the hen. Like the bigger bird, they instinctively search for and eat insects.

Preyed upon by almost everything with teeth and talons, the young turkeys transform the hen into the ultimate paranoid. At the first sign of danger the hen sounds an alarm putt that makes the mottled-brown chicks squat and freeze, easily blending in with their surroundings.

Like most wildlife, the hen displays amazing bravery when defending her young. Twice she fakes a broken wing to lead a coyote away from her hiding brood. Still, the brood is gradually shrinking in number.

Her job becomes easier with the turkeys' rapid growth. By the start of their third week the poults begin to get airborne and can roost on low-hanging limbs and bushes.

Food is abundant and seemingly without boundaries. The hen and poults spend a lot of time in a nearby farmfield, picking up grasshoppers and other insects that were munching on the crops. Like the hen, the poults will eat almost anything they can get in their mouths: greens, seeds, and maybe an occasional small lizard from a rock pile or crawfish from the shallow stream.

With the coming of autumn, the remaining young—two hens and a tom—are two-thirds the size of the hen. They still follow her as she feeds in the hardwoods, using their big feet to move the leaves that mask an assortment of wild nuts and insects.

As the days shorten and the weather cools, the hen and her young begin to mix in with similar flocks. Midwinter finds the flock concentrated around a harvested soybean field which, along with nearby acorns, provides their main source of food. Their feathers offer plenty of insulation from the cold. As long as they can reach food they will survive the winter.

A growing excitement spreads through the flock as spring approaches. The turkeys start to disperse and the toms begin to gobble and have shoving matches to reaffirm their places in the pecking order.

A veteran from springs past, the old hen takes the changes in stride. Her two female offspring are a little confused, but their befuddlement is minor compared to the mixed-up feelings of the young tom.

A mixed flock feeding in the fall. They often concentrate around harvested grainfields through late fall and winter. *Photo by Mike Blair.*

Now bigger than his mother, the jake basically looks the part of a tom. Unlike the dull brown of a hen, his feathers are black-tipped and shiny. Though rounded and dull, small spurs sprout from the backs of his legs. From his chest protrudes a stubby primitive feather known as a beard.

The young tom, called a jake, is at the awkward age of adolescence when hormones are raging through his young body but he's not totally sure what to do. Occasionally he gets so excited that he raises his body feathers, fans his uneven tail and maybe even cuts loose with a broken gobble.

Yet all too often his theatrics only get him in trouble. The bigger gobblers that tolerated him in the winter seem to take no greater pleasure than knocking the stuffing out of the smaller jake whenever he shows any signs of bravado.

He eventually mixes in with three of his own kind. Low birds on the totem pole, they mostly watch the spring ritual of replenishment from a distance. Once a hen lowers herself in front of the most dominant of the

A small flock of gobblers. Whether there are two or two dozen turkeys in a flock, each has his place in the pecking order. Knowing how to infringe on the pecking order is a good way to call turkeys. *Photo by Mike Blair.*

A strutting young gobbler, better known as a *jake*. Note the tail feathers, or *fan*. The immature tom has longer tail feathers in the middle and shorter ones on each side. An adult gobbler will have a completely even fan—tail feather lengths will be the same. *Photo by Ray Eye.*

Close-up of a jake's tail feathers. *Photo by Ray Eye.*

Turkeys

four. Another time they throw all caution aside and run to the calls of an unseen hen. The small flock is down to three after the loud bang rolls across the countryside.

The jake has it easy throughout the summer, obtaining food in much the same manner he did the year before as a poult. His body and features continue to fill out as autumn and then winter arrive. A full-fledged adult, the tom has few natural enemies, but persists in the paranoia that his mother taught him. The sights and sounds of man in his woods naturally seem to terrify him the most.

He spends the winter with several of his long-bearded counterparts. The ever-present pecking order keeps each bird in his place, yet they get along well. That is, they do until the combination of lengthening daylight and warm temperatures again begin to fill their minds with thoughts of love.

The toms become more and more agitated with each other's presence. Gobblers begin to challenge gobblers and fights are common.

From a distance it's tough to distinguish the two-year-old bird from older toms. His body is almost as large as theirs, as is his beard. Unlike

Juvenile gobblers will normally have shorter beards and spurs and be smaller in body size than adult gobblers. *Photo by Ray Eye.*

An adult gobbler in full strut displaying for the hens at mating time. Note how he has raised his feathers and pulled his head back into his body with his snood hanging down across his beak. *Photo by Ray Eye.*

the year before, he spends more time standing his ground and less time running.

The bird can hold his own against most two-year-old and some three-year-old gobblers, but he's no match for a couple of the real monarchs that rule the area. His spurs are three-quarters of an inch, and pointed but not terribly sharp, no match for the 1¼-inch curved spikes of the four- and five-year-olds.

That spring he scrounges a few hens to breed. The next year, the bird's third, is much better. He is one of the dominant birds in the pecking order, one that can be bullied by only a few other toms. He has his own little territory and many chicks come into the world carrying his genes.

As a four-year-old, the tom is the boss bird. Shortly after the winter flocks break up, he settles the matter with another big gobbler. The two close in on each other, gobbling challenges as they approach.

They bump bodies, flog each other and wrap their necks together in a tug of war. They also rise into the air time and time again, slashing at each other with their razor-sharp spurs. Finally the other gobbler retreats and the tom enjoys the best that the area has to offer—the best habitat and the most hens.

For a while the big gobbler is in the company of hens nearly all of the time. There are hens with him when he flies from his morning roost and even more come to his gobbles throughout the day.

And then his life slowly begins to change. The hens begin nesting and the still hot tom spends more and more time looking for new loves.

The gobbler is strutting in his favorite meadow one morning. The single hen that was with him at daybreak has gone to her nest and the tom is on his own.

On edge and excited, he gobbles at the sound of an owl hoot in the distance. Then, from up on the ridge come the sweet calls of hen. He first hears a few soft clucks and gentle yelps. The tom gobbles back, expecting the hen to come to him. But she doesn't and the next series of yelps comes from the same area.

The tom stands his ground for a while but a string of excited cutting and yelping is more than he can stand. He takes his time moving toward the hen, still expecting her to come running like all the rest.

The old patriarch stops to strut often, only to be coaxed onward by seductive promises. As he nears, the bird's ears pinpoint the source of the calls just over the lip of the ridge in front of him.

The tom steps over the break showing his finest strut. A soft putt pulls him from strut and he raises his head to look for the unseen hen that's been leading him on. . . .

3
Turkey Talk

The sport of turkey hunting seems to have an almost magical allure for those who try it. It's a tough feeling to convey, but there's no question that the calling is one of the prime attractions. I've often wondered if people would be fanatical about turkey hunting if it simply meant bushwacking for mute birds or taking them on the wing like oversized pheasants.

But luckily that's not how we hunt the best of all game birds. Turkeys are very vocal and spend a lot of time communicating with each other. Granted, it's not a language, but there are certain sounds that mean certain things. The more you understand the calls, the more you understand turkeys and what it takes to get in on the conversation.

Obviously there's no way I can use ink and paper to copy the calls of wild turkeys. What I can do, however, is take a little time to explain their system of communication.

Hens

Yelp

The yelp is unquestionably the most universal of all turkey sounds, yet it's also the call that sees the greatest amount of variance.

Though the basic call sounds like the word "calk," hens use yelps as the basis of a wide variety of calls. In my opinion, the way the yelp is expressed gives the call its true meaning.

For instance, hens often use real soft, low yelps to convey a sense of security. They yelp like this when feeding, when waking up on the roost in the morning (commonly known as tree yelping), and in just about any other situation when things are calm.

But the yelps sound totally different when the hen is trying to express some excitement—such as when she wants to get mated in the worst sort of way.

The mating yelp is a call that's often full of excitement and desire. It's definitely louder than the soft yelps of contentment. The degree of excitement and the length of the mating call vary not only from bird to bird, but also from time to time.

No two turkeys sound or call alike. Some turkey hunters say that a mating yelp numbers three to six yelps. What they forget is that turkeys can't count.

I've heard hens going to a gobbler putting no more than two or three yelps together. On the same ridge I've heard a hen yelp nonstop as she runs to a gobbler. The next day the hens may exchange styles, the quiet one becoming a blabbermouth and vice versa. It all depends on how they're feeling.

Hens often use yelps for locating each other. Again, how they feel determines how they sound. If they want only to check in with another bird they may sound just a couple of unexcited yelps.

If they've been separated from an old friend that they're trying to find, you can often hear the panic in their long string of yelps. Likewise, you can hear the anger in the yelps of a dominant hen that's flustered with a bird challenging her place at the top of the pecking order.

Cluck

Like the soft yelp, the short and soft cluck is a basic call of contentment. Hens use it to keep track of each other, but I've heard lone hens clucking as if they're just trying to reassure themselves.

As with the yelp, the number of consecutive clucks varies from bird to bird and from circumstance to circumstance. Hens often cluck to communicate a feeling of ease with nearby turkeys. A feeding hen may cluck only once or twice, while a hen caught deep in the grasp of passion may cluck fast and almost continuously to the gobbler that's courting her.

Putt

Many people associate putting with alarmed turkeys, but turkeys will putt, or "pop" as some call it, under a variety of conditions. They may start putting loudly when they're spooked, but they can make the same sounds when they're excited for other reasons, like anger or pleasure.

Cackle

A cackle is a string of snappy, excited calls that starts low, rises, then comes back down again. Most of the cackling I've heard hens do was excited cutting rather than yelps.

Cutting

Cutting is actually a string of very aggressive and very loud putting. Its rhythm is fast and full of excitement. Hens often cut as they're flying off the roost in the morning and when they're getting impatient trying to find a gobbler. A hen that's challenging another hen for placement in the pecking order can also do a lot of excited cutting.

Purrs

A rolling, almost vibrating call, purring usually means contentment. It is soft communication. Like most calls it can be long and drawn out or short and quick. Feeding hens often purr as they peck at food. Sometimes the purring is so soft hunters can't hear it unless they're within twenty or thirty yards.

But as with most calls, purring can also be loud and sometimes aggressive. Hens often purr a lot when they've been separated and are trying to regroup.

Two hens getting ready to settle a dispute — over their places in the pecking order or anything else — can start purring hard, long, and loud as their excitement builds.

Kee-Kee

The kee-kee is the real lost call of the wild turkeys. Almost the only time you hear the whistling kee-kee is when turkeys are trying to regroup. This call is almost always full of excitement and often panic as the birds hurry to find each other.

All of the Above

As you can tell, there isn't any one call that precisely expresses whatever a turkey is trying to communicate. An excited hen might yelp, putt, cut, and purr to get a gobbler's attention. Chances are, she'll do a combination of two or more calls to get her point across.

Those who have listened to real hens excitedly calling to gobblers will tell you that it's rare for a hen to simply yelp. A hen's calls often change as the excitement builds.

For instance, a hen may start off with a few clucks or mellow yelps when she's looking for a tom. When she gets a response her yelps may become snappier in rhythm, louder, and longer. As time passes and her agitation increases, she may send out a string of excited cuts and a few enthusiastic yelps. She may eventually forget all about the yelps and use nothing but cutting.

On the other hand, another hen may stick mainly to yelps while filling in with some soothing clucks and purrs to find a tom. No two turkeys call alike.

Toms

Gobble

A tom's gobble is the most exhilarating and misunderstood of all turkey calls. Many people think that gobbling is a sign of the spring mating season. While toms do gobble then, that's far from the only time they gobble.

The gobble is a call of pure excitement and intensity. I've heard it all twelve months of the year. In the fall the gobble can be a gathering call for a dispersed flock of mature bachelor longbeards. Any time of year it is a sign of excitement.

Several autumns ago I watched a flock of eight gobblers trying to squeeze through a small hole in a woven wire fence. First one bird would try and then another. Eventually the birds started bumping into each other.

Soon I saw a tail fan out; minutes later a couple of birds began strutting to show their dominance. As the frenzy built, the toms began to gobble back and forth at each other. By the time it was over all eight birds were standing and gobbling at each other. They continued nonstop for close to twenty minutes.

The reason we hear the most gobbling in the spring is because it's the season of the most excitement. Toms are gobbling back and forth as they jockey for their places in the pecking order. The gobble is also their gathering call to round up willing hens.

Often any hint of surprise or excitement can get a tom to fire off a gobble. The shrill calling of a crow, the deep hoots of an owl, and a clap of thunder are all regular sources of inspiration.

When the hormones are charging through a bird's body at full speed, who knows what they'll gobble at? I once hunted a big longbeard in a patch of hardwoods that wasn't far from a small country school. The kids got a softball game going at midmorning. Even a half-mile away I could follow the progress of the game by the loud, enthusiastic screams of the children. Most times the shrieks that followed a good hit would be answered with a resounding gobble.

And it's been my experience that toms will start gobbling at a younger age than some people believe. I've seen jakes—year-old toms—stand in one spot and gobble almost nonstop for close to an hour. I don't think even they know why they're doing it.

I've also heard young-of-the-year birds doing their best gobble when they get excited. Sometimes it sounds more like a hacking cough than a gobble.

Yelp and Other Calls

Most hunters are so infatuated with the gobble of a tom that they either don't know or simply forget about the rest of the calls in the bearded bird's vocabulary.

Gobblers use yelps much the way hens do. Their yelps range from the soft sounds of contentment to the excited yelps of a fall bird inquiring about the new bird on the block.

Like the gobble, the yelp is part of the tom's vocabulary throughout the year. Even though it is most commonly associated with the fall and winter, I've had full-grown gobblers come yelping to spring hen calls.

Jakes are especially notorious for yelping a reply in the spring. Sometimes the response is a string of pure yelps, but sometimes it includes both yelps and gobbles, or sometimes straight gobbles. It all depends on the bird and what he's feeling at the time.

Toms use the cluck as well as the soft purr to convey that they are at ease. Two toms ready to square off for a fight can sound aggressive purrs and loud putts to communicate a feeling of pure hate. They often use loud cutting to accomplish the same thing.

Most of the time the calls of a tom are slightly more drawn out and coarse than those of a hen. But I've seen a big longbeard open his mouth and let out a string of yelps as clear and sweet as cold spring water. From a distance I would have sworn I was listening to a young hen.

Pardon the repetition, but each bird is different.

Spit and Drum

Even though it's not exactly a call, there's one last gobbler sound that's important to hunting—what's known as the spit and drum of a strutting tom. It's normally heard from an approaching gobbler in the spring: a deep hum that in some ways sounds like a distant truck mired in the mud. The closer the gobbler gets, the louder it sounds. This one noise does more for my pulse than any in turkey hunting.

The sounds are made when the gobbler snaps in and out of full strut. The sharp hiss of the spit and the low, vibrating sound of the drumming can be heard from a distance of up to sixty yards.

It can be a tough sound to describe and many beginners have trouble hearing it. I often encourage new hunters to spend some time listening to strutting tame turkeys. Once you hear it, you'll never forget it.

4
Talking Turkey

As a boy I learned that the first step to calling a wild turkey is simply being able to sound like one. Time after time I'd hear a gobbler that had ignored my calls open up to the first calls of a hen. At the time I wanted to make those sounds more than anything else in the world.

I went to great lengths to learn how to talk with the turkeys. I'd belly-crawl through wet leaves and muck to get within hearing distance of a flock of turkeys. I'd follow them all day and then go home and mimic them all night.

Back in the early 1960s there weren't many turkey callers tucked away in the Ozarks, but I made it my business to meet them all. Just hearing a rumor about somebody bagging a gobbler would have me begging a ride to hear every last detail of the hunt, especially how the hunter had called.

Things are a lot easier for the novice turkey hunter these days. There are more turkeys in the woods to listen to. Or a hunter can take the easier route by watching videos or listening to tapes of good callers.

There's no better place to hear good calling than at a calling contest. You can hear caller after caller giving his best shot at imitating nearly every call in a turkey's vocabulary.

Since their inception, calling contests have come under attack from some turkey hunters. They say that the stage and the woods are two different places, that callers skillful in contests can't impress "the real judges in the woods." It's been written that fancy calling has no place in the wild and that the good woodsmanship of a local boy could best the skills of a calling champion time after time.

It's true that good calling isn't worth much if the hunter doesn't know a turkey track from a racetrack. But combine really good calling with good woodsmanship and you have a combination that can't be beat.

Champion callers like Terry Rohm, Preston Pittman, Billy MaCoy, Walter Parrott, and Paul Butski are also some of the best turkey hunters in the nation. They often follow the spring seasons like migrant workers follow ripening crops — and their harvest success rates in states they've never seen is outstanding.

All of these well-known hunters will tell you that good calling is a large part of their success. They all encourage hunters to learn every call that they can. The last decade has seen a lot of change in the turkey woods. There's more hunting pressure from improving callers, and turkeys are exposed to more man-made calling than ever before. Being the best caller you can is becoming more important.

There are times when you don't need to be an advanced caller. If the hens are all nesting, the weather fair and the hunting pressure light, a few yelps and clucks may be all it takes.

But when the weather is off, hunters are behind every tree, or the hens are clinging nymphomaniacs, it will take good calling to work birds into range. Many times I've seen good callers consistently take turkeys while average callers emerge from the woods without success.

Ask a hundred different turkey hunters and you'll probably get a hundred different theories on calling. I'll be the first to admit that my ideas don't agree with what is gospel to some people. But I know what's worked for me and the many turkey hunters I've taught down through the years.

One of the most important ideas to remember is that each turkey has its own feelings and personality. I've never seen any two turkeys act the same, nor have I ever found any calling methods that work all of the time. You have to be able to recognize what it takes to turn on different turkeys in different situations.

In my second year of turkey hunting I came upon a magazine out in my grandparents' outhouse that contained an article on turkey hunting. It said the *only* way to call in a gobbler was to yelp three times, wait ten minutes, yelp three more times, and so on.

The next morning I walked up to a ridge where I knew a gobbler roosted. At daybreak the tom gobbled and I closed the distance. I pulled a watch out of one pocket, my call out of another, and made three yelps.

The gobbler hammered back a gobble but I sat silently and stared at the watch. After ten minutes I yelped three more times and the bird started gobbling harder. Then from my left came the yelps and cuts of a real hen turkey.

The more she called, the more the tom gobbled. The more the tom gobbled, the more excited she became. Within minutes the hen was calling almost nonstop. The tom flew from the roost and went right to the hen. They were gone. "Hey wait a minute," I thought. "My ten minutes isn't even up yet."

It was obvious: that was a gobbler that liked his ladies loud and demanding.

But you won't know what a turkey wants until you spend some time feeling him out. I usually advise hunters to start off calling simple and short. If you make a couple of clucks, a bird runs in gobbling and you have to peel him off your leg, then you obviously didn't need anything else.

Make your first series of calls very soft. A turkey can hear even the softest tree yelps from an amazing distance when the woods are quiet in the early morning.

If a gobbler is either not responding or responding but not moving closer, then start increasing your intensity. Try a longer and louder string of yelps. If that doesn't work, add some cutting to your yelps. You may end up having to make long strings of excited cutting to get a bird to come in.

How often should you call? That's a good question and one that's impossible to answer because turkeys don't wear watches. If you can keep a gobbler interested with well-spaced calls, then you may be able to stick with it and get him.

But I've always been an aggressive caller. There are times when pouring it on hot and heavy is the only way to bring a bird into range.

My last Oklahoma hunt with Terry Funk coincided with some of the worst hunting conditions in history. The birds weren't in their normal hangouts, nor were they responding well to calls.

Terry and I were working a riverbottom when a tom gobbled at my cutting. Not sure where the bird was, I stayed in the thick tamaracks while Terry sat near the edge of the trees.

My first series of yelps got no response, but by building to some serious cutting I got the gobbler to sound off and eventually come in. The longbeard finally glided across the tiny river and I shot him as he came through the tamaracks.

Later in the afternoon we got another single response but my yelps failed to get the turkey to sound off again. I eventually built to a series of about thirty excited yelps before I got another answer. But the bird still didn't seem to be getting any closer.

To make a long story short, the one turkey we were calling was part of a mixed flock of a few toms and a lot of hens that showed some interest in real excited cutting. So that's what I did — almost nonstop cutting for about forty-five minutes. In turn, the turkeys yelped, cut, and gobbled with the same intensity.

The dominant gobbler gave us the slip but Terry was able to drop a longbeard from the flock when it finally got within range.

Try not to use the same exact call time after time. Vary it a yelp or two each time to make it more authentic. Try to convey a feeling in your calls. Try to become a turkey.

Here's an example: I'm in the woods and a gobbler responds to my owl hoot from about three hundred yards away. Depending on the terrain, I'll move to within about two hundred yards, set up, and let out a few soft clucks and yelps, suggesting, "I'm kind of lonely; is anybody out there?"

If the bird responds I'll move a little closer and use a few more yelps to imply a hen that's cutting the distance and saying, "I'd like to meet you, where are you at?"

That may be all it takes. If the gobbler acts as if he's coming in, I use the same basic call to say, "Glad you're coming to see me; come on in."

But if the gobbler won't budge or shows some hesitation, I step up the yelps and perhaps preface them with excited putts implying, "I'm really wanting to get together . . . soon!"

If the tom shows a little more interest but is taking too much time coming in, I may start the next call with some good cutting followed by the yelps. I'm trying to say, "Come on up and see me, big boy . . . and HURRY!"

If I think he's still not working fast enough I may eventually end up using some very aggressive and excited cutting. Sorry, but we can't print what I'm promising the gobbler.

Take a little time to think over the situation when you're having trouble getting a turkey to gobble at or come to your calls. Sometimes one small variation can make a big difference.

Sometimes people call too loudly. Extremely loud yelps and cutting work well in stiff winds but may be little more than locating calls when it's calm. If you think you may have called too loudly, change calling sites and then start from scratch, only softer. If you're at all close they'll probably still hear you.

One perfectly still morning before turkey hunting season I was walking a logging road while I worked on a troublesome mouth call. I gave a few real soft yelps that were really just loud enough for me to hear well. A turkey gobbled from about three hundred yards away.

"What a coincidence," I thought. A minute or so later I tried the same call and the same bird gobbled back. I waited a few minutes later and called again. That time the gobble was closer.

Changing the mechanical call you're using can sometimes get a bird turned on, especially if your skill with a diaphragm call is average and the area you're hunting has lots of pressure. Change positions on the bird, pull out a box or slate call, and you may have the bird eating out of your hand.

It was late morning when Jack Hessler and I set out to work a good turkey that lived in some heavily hunted timber. Knowing that most hunters were coming from the east and using excited diaphragm calls, Jack and I circled around to the west.

Using my box call, I gave three or four soft, raspy yelps. A coarse gobble sounded in front of us. After fifteen minutes I gave a similar call and he was closer.

We played it soft and easy, calling only four times in the hour it took the bird to close the 350 yards between us. Jack took the 24½-pound gobbler at twenty yards. The old gobbler's longest spur measured 1¾ inches.

It is also possible to call too often. It sounds strange, but there are times when a gobbler gets too worked up to come in. Sometimes when you simply go silent, the turkey comes looking for you anywhere from twenty minutes to two hours later.

Too many hunters concentrate on calling only from hen to gobbler. If the tom's not coming in, do some experimenting. He may have some lady friends; try some challenging hen calls.

If you can't get a gobbler interested in romance, maybe you can toss some insults at him. Make your calls raspier and more drawn-out—like those of another gobbler or jake. When the spring comes late and the toms are more concerned with dominance than mating, sounding like a smart aleck can really get on the nerves of a cocky longbeard.

The main thing to remember is to approach calling with an open mind and to be prepared for anything. If the hunt isn't going well, try some of the more advanced calls, such as aggressive cutting and the gobbler or jake yelps. You have nothing to lose but much to gain.

And no doubt the best way to learn is to actually get out and call in turkeys. Use common sense. Don't get out and call just before the season; you'll spook the birds. In fact, it's probably best to simply listen the last week before the season. Calling after the season is also good practice.

Be sure you don't go to the same place every day to call the turkeys, especially on public ground. Go often enough to get your confidence up, but again, use your common sense.

5
Calling Devices

I can still see Grandma sitting on the front porch, rocking back and forth in a creaking chair as she peeled a pan of potatoes she'd gotten from the root cellar. To pass the time she'd often sing or hum an old tune that had probably been around the hills as long as the old homestead.

But I liked it best when she'd talk with the turkeys. To a wide-eyed child of no more than six it was amazing. She'd just open her mouth and out would come the yelps of an old hen. Talking turkey was so natural for her that the old chair never missed a beat and Grandma never slowed with the "taters." Yet her sounds wouldn't have been as impressive if not for the yelps and gobbles that responded from the hills around her.

I can also remember asking Grandpa over and over to tell me about the times in his younger years when he called turkeys—to shoot and eventually to eat. Throughout each story I'd beg him to repeat the very sounds he'd used.

Sometimes he'd call with his voice; other times he'd use an old blackboard slate. In one of my favorite stories he chalked the stock of his old shotgun, then produced yelps and purrs by pulling a wooden striker along the old Winchester.

I sometimes wonder what Grandma and Grandpa would think of the turkey calls of today, not only because there are so many but also because

An eastern wild turkey gobbling at what he thinks is a hen available for mating. There are a variety of artificial calling devices that a turkey hunter can choose from to lure the tom into gun range. *Photo by Ray Eye.*

they are so easy to use. No longer is turkey calling something that is mastered after years of sheer repetition, whether for simple entertainment or for feeding a growing family.

Modern technology has done a great deal to refine a practice begun hundreds of years ago by American Indians. Today's turkey hunters have it much better than hunters of even a decade ago. There are more calls available and they're much easier to use. Nevertheless, it's tough for someone to walk into a sporting goods store, pick up any call and be able to call in a turkey by the time he leaves. Calling still takes practice and a good knowledge of the basics.

I really can't say that one particular call, or family of calls for that matter, is better than the others. Each individual has to find the kind of call that gives him the most comfort and confidence.

Personally, I like them all. You can bet that I'll have a half-dozen mouth calls, a good quality slate call, and my old faithful box call. Each call has its place in turkey hunting. It's not unusual for me to use all three — the slate, box, and mouth calls — on the same day.

I usually tell a beginner to start with a box or slate call, then to try another call as soon as he feels comfortable with the first. Even experi-

Calling Devices 55

enced hunters should have the common sense to be versatile with all kinds of calls.

The day will come when the gobbler that's ignored your diaphragm calls will all but run you over when you try a friction call. Not a season goes by that I'm not trying something new to the market. There's no doubt that being skilled with all kinds of calls has added to my success.

Of the two types of calls—air and friction calls—there's not much doubt that the friction is the easier to use. As the name implies, sounds are generated by rubbing two materials together. With the right materials and some practice, those calls should sound like a turkey.

Slate Calls

Ever since my grandpa laid that first call made of broken chalkboard slate and a corncob-and-cedar striker in my hand, slate calls have always had a special place in my heart. The fact that I've used slate calls to call in hundreds of turkeys has also helped endear them to me.

Over the years I've used the soft, natural notes of slate to call in toms that seemed a little call-shy. In 1988 I was hunting Merriams late in the

The corn cob and slate is a very realistic-sounding friction call, excellent for soft tree calls, purrs, and clucks. Never lift the striker off the calling surface when making a call. *Photo by Ray Eye.*

season in a heavily hunted area with mixed results. On my third morning I moved in close to a roosted flock and used an old slate to send a gobbler soft tree yelps, followed by excited cutting.

Another hunter who was set up nearby was using a mouth call, but the tom wasn't interested. By the time morning flydown arrived I had the bird in a gobbling frenzy. A friend killed the longbeard as he came running in.

For years the basic materials for making slate calls were similar to the homemade call that got me started. About the only variable was the handle that held the peg. Sometimes it was hollow wood and sometimes hollow corncob.

Then came plexiglass instead of cedar in the striker to waterproof the call and make it sound more consistent. It was a heck of an idea and it worked well.

Then a few years ago people started experimenting with new materials to replace the slate. Today you can find "slates" made of aluminum, glass, plexiglass, acrylic, and almost any combination thereof. Slate calls can also be stacked in double and triple layers.

It seems as if every manufacturer has its own striker/slate combination of varying dimensions and materials. They all sound different.

Generally speaking, the old-fashioned wood and true slate calls sound rather mellow. They are great for soft and sweet yelps and purrs. Their only drawback, besides not being waterproof, is a lack of volume for locating gobblers or for windy days.

Some of the new materials don't seem to have the gentle finesse of the old materials. Don't get me wrong; they still sound good, but to me the soft talk isn't quite as sweet. But the up side is that the glass and acrylic calls have plenty of volume. They can make good yelps and almost anyone can use them to imitate cutting.

It's up to the individual to choose his best slate call. If you're in the market for a good slate call I'd suggest that you look around and listen. Check with local turkey hunters to see what they favor and ask them to give you a demonstration to see how their calls sound.

Try to get your hands on as many types of slate calls as possible. You have to be physically comfortable with a call to get the most out of it. Naturally you'll want to see how easy it is to get turkey sounds from the call. The easier it is, the faster you'll learn everything, from the basics through the advanced calls.

Once you've decided on a call, the next step is to learn how to use it properly. The first and probably most important step is to start getting good, consistent sounds from the call. Don't worry about the fancy stuff yet. That will come later.

If you're right-handed you'll want to hold the slate in your left hand. Most of today's calls come with a sound chamber already built onto the bottom of the slate. If so, just hold the call as you would a can of soda pop, in close to your body.

If you have a chamberless call, it becomes important to create a good sound chamber with your hand and fingers. Again, you'll want to tuck the call in close to your body.

Hold the striker in your other hand, much as you would a pencil. Grasp the striker about an inch or two from the bottom for better control and consistency.

Place the striker near the center of the slate at a slight angle and softly draw it toward you. Go slowly at first, experimenting until you get a feel for the amount of pressure it takes to get the right notes. Once you've got the feel for the call, start moving the striker far enough to create a yelp.

Once you get a smooth, continuous sound from the call, it's time to start putting notes together. One of the biggest mistakes people make is lifting the striker from the call's surface. Keep the striker on the surface. I like to go back and forth in a straight line, but some calls sound better if you move the striker in a circular motion. Try it both ways until you find the best approach for you and your call.

Once you're able to put two notes together, try three notes, four, and so on. Strive for consistency and remember that the turkey rhythm starts off soft and short before building to longer and louder yelps.

In my opinion the slate call produces the most realistic purrs of any call. The purr is also the easiest sound to produce. You simply draw the peg across the slate slowly, using different amounts of pressure until you achieve the sound. Chances are, you were purring when you were trying to get your first sounds from the slate.

Making the cluck is just the opposite. Place the striker on the slate and snap it toward you, moving it no more than a quarter- to a half-inch. Use more pressure than you did for the purr and don't lift the striker from the call.

Cutting on a slate is a lot easier to do than it is to explain in a book. It's actually fast and hard clucks. Once you've mastered the yelps and clucks and have heard some good cutting on a tape or from a good caller, combining the two into excited cutting will come easily.

Since you have to hold some models of slate calls close to your body, it is important for you to practice from authentic calling positions. Try sitting with your back against a tree. If you feel too cramped with the call against your abdomen, you can often move it to the inside of your leg.

Once you're consistently getting good sounds from the call, practice calling with your eyes straight ahead. You won't want to be looking down at the call when a big gobbler comes walking in.

As you get better, start experimenting with the hand holding the call. Even with calls that come with sound chambers you'll be able to vary your calls by opening and closing your hand. Also, learn how to call purrs, clucks, and yelps as softly as possible.

The biggest complaint I've heard about the slate call is that it takes two hands and some movement to use. Some hunters claim that it spooks birds. It might, if used at the wrong time, but I've never had such a problem.

The key is to keep the call low and close to your body so that your raised legs will conceal the movement. There's really less motion involved than you think; you need to move only a few fingers. If the problem persists, you can try making a camouflaged apron that hangs from your belt.

If you've chosen your calling site well, the turkey shouldn't be able to see you until he's within range. By the time the gobbler is close enough to see any call movement, you should already have the call down and the gun up and ready to go.

I like to angle the gun across my lap, the forearm resting on a raised knee and the butt on the ground. When it comes time to move for the gun all you have to do is let the call rest on your lap and slowly move your hands to your gun. If you can see the turkey, wait to grab your gun until his head goes behind an obstruction like a tree, blowdown, or fanned tail.

Like any sound-producing instrument, slate calls require a little special care. The main objective is to protect the slate surface from any material that might fill in its pores, such as dirt, dust, or even the oil from your fingertips.

To get the best sound, you'll want to keep the slate surface slightly rough with a little sand paper or emery cloth. Don't go overboard; all it needs is an occasional brisk sanding.

How often you'll need to sand will vary from call to call. You definitely need to sand daily and every time the surface gets dirty or smoothed from being carried unprotected in a coat pocket. I also like to sand the call if it looks as if I'm going to be in one spot for a long time. The last thing you want is the sound to start to go when a gobbler is only halfway in.

When using one of the old-style cedar-pegged calls in high humidity or even rain, carry the call in some sort of plastic bag. If conditions are really wet you can leave the call in the bag and carry on. The sound will be muted, but surprisingly effective. But that's the way it is with slate calls. They work. I really can't understand a turkey hunter who doesn't own and know how to use one.

Taking proper care of your calling devices is important. Always keep your slate well sanded and don't touch calling surfaces with your fingers. *Photo by Ray Eye.*

Box Calls

Even more so than slate calls, box calls are viewed by many turkey hunters as things meant only for beginners. In fact, a few years ago a writer questioned my hunting capabilities when I said I'd be using a box call. By noon he was wanting to know where he could buy one.

Box calls have as much going for them as any turkey call. They're relatively easy to use, they can get loud for locating or whisper quiet for soft talk, and they'll produce almost every call in a turkey's vocabulary.

But the most important thing is that they simply sound like turkeys. Most professional turkey hunters can easily tell the difference between a diaphragm call and a real turkey. But put someone that's good with a box call in the woods and the pros may end up scratching their heads and guessing.

The box call can have the same effect on turkeys, especially those that have become accustomed to hunters using mouth calls. Several years ago Ben Held and I headed to South Dakota's Black Hills for a try at Merriams.

The push-button yelper is an excellent beginner's device because it is so easy to use. Many experienced hunters also use this device because it makes some very authentic sounds. *Photo by Ray Eye.*

The little set of hills that we hunted was full of signs of both turkeys and turkey hunters. We heard some gobbling at sunrise but it was as if the birds had a case of lock-beak when I opened up with my diaphragm calls at fly-down time. It got so bad that I began to get a complex.

Then I pulled out my weathered old box call and gave a few clucks and excited yelps. Suddenly everything changed. In scarcely more than one day of hunting I called in eight different longbeards using the box call, while the diaphragm call struck out.

That's not the first time box calls have saved me, nor will it be the last. They're simply deadly, deadly calls if you know how to use them.

The principle of the box call involves drawing a wooden paddle over a wooden rectangular box. The friction created should sound like a turkey.

For years most box calls looked pretty much the same, the paddle hinged to a box, which was usually made of cedar or sometimes walnut. There are also smaller box calls with unattached lids on the market.

Some manufacturers have started using acrylic for call parts to prevent moisture from changing a call's tone. Since the sound is still created by wood on wood, the acrylic-containing calls are often good.

Although most box calls on the market may look alike, they sure don't sound alike. Some are good and some are not so good. The only

Calling Devices

way to know for sure is to check with local experts and do some experimenting.

Most stores will let you take a brand out of the box and give it a few tries. If you can get away with it, try every darned call that they have. Sounds not only vary from brand to brand, but to some extent from call to call. Listen well for what sounds the best.

Move the paddle slowly across the box's edge when trying a new call. Feel whether it moves smoothly and look closely to see if it makes consistent contact with the box. If a box call can make very soft sounds it's probably tuned properly.

Once you've picked a call it's time to start some serious practice. As with the slate, start with the basics; simply get a smooth note from the call.

You'll usually want to start with the middle of the lid resting on the edge of the box, using just a little pressure to bring the lid toward the call. Try a few starting points and vary amounts of pressure on the lid until you come up with the best sound.

If you're having problems, or even if you're not, you may want to experiment with the way you hold the call. Most hunters hold the box horizontally with the lid on top, but that might not work best for you. Some use the call horizontally with the paddle down.

For years I've had success with holding the call vertically, the hinge down. Others do well with the hinge up. Most people run the lid against the box but there are some who hold the lid still and scrape with the box. Try all methods and decide what's best for you.

Which wall of a two-sided box you use can be another variable. Try both sides to find out which one sounds better. Some calls have sides of different thicknesses. The thicker of the two makes the deeper notes.

Some such box calls claim that one side is for hen notes and the other for gobbler yelps. Don't let that worry you. Either side will work for hen calls. Anyone who has listened to many turkeys has stories of hens with deep and raspy calls. If the "gobbler" side sounds best—go ahead and use it. Neither you nor the gobblers will be disappointed.

Once you've developed your own style and consistent notes, it's time to get a little more ambitious. Go from one good note to a string of yelps. Make sure you have the ever-important turkey rhythm, and try for high and low notes in each individual sound.

Purring on a box call is as easy as slowly drawing the lid across the box. The key is to do it smoothly. Clucks are just short, snappy yelps.

Be sure to practice both ends of the volume spectrum. There will be times when the wind is howling and you'll be working the box and lid like a set of hedge clippers just to be heard.

Making the soft yelps, purrs, and clucks is probably more important.

Try to get so soft that you can barely hear the sound. At that point a turkey could still probably hear the call at sixty yards. If you're having difficulty calling softly, you might stuff some tissue or a cotton glove in the chamber of the box.

Reducing movement while calling is easily accomplished. As with the slate, practice calling from a sitting position with the call between your body and your raised knees. By keeping your arms tucked into your sides, you'll need only a little hand movement.

Paying attention and having a good calling sight should give you plenty of time to drop the call and lift the stock of your shotgun. Thinking back, I can't recall ever spooking a turkey just because I was using a box call.

But simply walking through the woods with the call in your pocket can get you into trouble; the lid scrapes noisily back and forth, making a variety of obnoxious noises. Stuffing the box with a tissue or glove can help solve the problem. Using a tight rubberband to hold the lid down tight would be yet another solution.

Keeping a box call sounding its best is largely a matter of keeping the calling surfaces clean of dirt, mud, oil, and other foreign substances. Another necessity is keeping the lid and edge of the box well chalked with a soft, oil-free chalk. For safety reasons it's best to use the specially-made brown box-call chalk rather than the white and blue chalk you can buy at hardware stores.

I like to chalk my box call first thing in the morning and again later if I'm going to be using it for any length of time. You can usually check the bottom of the lid to see when it needs a little more chalk. Always chalk the lip of the box while you're at it.

Occasionally, perhaps once a year, you might want to use some light sandpaper or emery cloth to clean the lid and lip of your box call. Take your time; go gently enough that you don't scrape deep into the wood.

If you're hunting in the rain or high humidity it's important to keep the box call as dry as possible. Carrying the call in a plastic bag between calling sights will help. If conditions get really wet you can use the call inside the bag.

I know it sounds as if box calls can be something of a problem. But hey, you ought to look at it from the turkey's point of view.

Mouth Calls

Turkey hunters have been using their mouths to fool turkeys for centuries. Indians used their bare voices and sucked on an old turkey wing bone to call birds.

I've used pipe stems, soda straws, and ink pens to call gobblers. A good friend, Damon Jarvis, could put most calls and callers to shame with a wild cherry leaf.

But mouth calls, commonly known as diaphragm calls, are without a doubt the most popular calls in the turkey woods today. Some hunters say they like them because they leave both hands free for handling the gun. Others choose them because they're compact. The pure challenge of mastering the call is yet another reason for the diaphragm call's popularity.

There are several theories about the origin of diaphragm calls, but I guess the theories aren't as important as how the calls work. Most mouth calls consist of a piece of latex stretched tight between a folded aluminum horseshoe that's covered with a piece of tape. Air blown over the call causes the latex to vibrate rapidly, and those vibrations can be transformed into turkey calls.

Sounds simple, doesn't it? Those who have been around the calls for a couple of decades will tell you that it's not nearly as simple as it used to be.

Originally all diaphragm calls consisted of a single reed. I can remember making my own single-reed calls by cutting up condoms and stretching the latex between plumber's lead in the late 1960s.

Even back then I didn't think much of the single-reed calls. The calls worked, but to me they never quite sounded like real turkeys.

Later someone tried using two pieces of latex, one stretched slightly behind the other. That development got me much more interested in diaphragm calls and I spent more and more time cutting condoms and lead. Multiple-reed mouth calls could be made to sound like turkeys and weren't too hard to use. Things really snowballed from there.

Obviously the next step up in complexity was the triple-reed call. When necessary it produces more volume, but is still capable of good soft talk in the hands of a skilled caller. I've always considered it a call for the intermediate to advanced caller.

There are also mouth calls with four — or even more — reeds on the market, but I really question whether they have many advantages for most turkey hunters. To be honest, I rarely use them myself.

Then hunters started discovering the advantages of split reeds. I'm talking about calls with either slits or even large holes in the longest, uppermost reed.

The first time I heard such a call was quite by accident years ago. Mike Held and I were hunting when Mike stopped and tried to separate the reeds on his call with his fingers. As luck (and I do mean luck) would have it, one of the reeds tore. Mike cussed a little but threw the call in anyway. Both of our eyes lit up like neon signs when we heard his new call. Suddenly I started ripping many of my favorite calls.

The rips make the latex vibrate even more, giving the call every bit as much rasp as a cranked-up hen turkey. The larger the slit or tear, the raspier the call. It's a sound that's popular with turkeys and turkey hunters alike.

There are basically two kinds of slits in diaphragm calls. One is actually a pair of tiny slits, one on each edge of the call. These calls are usually double reeds; they're easy to use, yet have a raspy tone.

The other kind is made by removing a chunk of latex about as big as a pencil eraser from the upper reed. The most common calls were originally triple or quadruple reeds, known as 2.5 and 3.5 respectively. They offer more than enough rasp but can be a little tough for some people to blow.

Just when the cut calls started becoming popular, yet another style of diaphragm call was introduced. Some callers are getting good sounds from these calls, which put each reed within its own frame. (The original calls stretched the reeds across one single frame.) Such calls can make some good sounds but may feel a little awkward and chunky in the mouths of many hunters.

Combine all of the possibilities of multiple- and cut-reed calls with the two sizes that most major call manufacturers produce and you have quite a selection of calls out there. In fact, there are so many that it's starting to get confusing for beginning and intermediate callers.

As mentioned earlier, I really don't care for the sounds of single-reed calls. Even though they're fairly easy to blow I don't recommend them for beginners, even though a lot of toms are called in with these thin calls every year. For just a little extra effort the double-reed call has much more to offer.

The double-reed call is still, and probably always will be, the best all-around call on the market. It is absolutely the easiest to learn on and is easily blown, and it can produce a wide range of turkey sounds for most hunters.

I suggest that most beginners get started with a double-reed call. Once they feel comfortable with it they can move to a double-reed that has a pair of tiny slits, which is still easy to handle yet sounds realistic.

Probably the next step would be a 2.5. It can take a little getting used to, but once a hunter has it down there's not a call he can't make in the woods.

The level of skill a hunter reaches is just a matter of personal preference. I know many excellent callers who stick with the double, raspy double, and the 2.5 for all of their calling.

This may sound strange if you haven't tried it, but possibly the hardest part of learning to use a diaphragm call is simply being able to tolerate the call resting on the roof of the mouth. The body naturally doesn't want to tolerate something that large near the throat; many people gag.

Everyone has to break himself in at his own pace. I believe that too many people expect things to happen too quickly. For most people learning to use a mouth call isn't something to start a week or two before the season.

It's best to begin by simply holding the call between your lips for a while. Next, move the call inward so that it's between your teeth and cheek at the side of your mouth.

If that's no problem, then try to put the call on the roof of your mouth, the open end facing out and the call far enough forward that the front of the frame rests against the back of your gums. Be sure that the longest reed is at the top. Hold it in place for a few seconds if you can. Then remove your fingers and try shutting your mouth as you hold the call in place with the middle of your tongue.

If the call simply won't fit (the frame is too big), you may want to try a smaller call. If the frame will fit but the call still feels too big, then you may want to take some scissors and start trimming the tape from around the call. Take it easy when you cut; remove only a hair at a time until the call will fit in place.

There are some people who have no problems tolerating the call in their mouths. I've seen a person slip a call into his mouth for the first time without any negative reaction. Some people need months to get used to the feel, and others gag every time.

Hunters who simply can't handle a diaphragm needn't worry. The friction, slate, and box calls can be just as effective and are actually easier to use. Someone who wants the sound of a mouth call can switch to a tube call, which is actually the same latex stretched over a plastic tube. The call rests on the outside of your mouth, so wouldn't cause any gagging.

Once you can hold a diaphragm inside your mouth, it's time to start working on making some sort of noise. First, make sure the call is properly fitted against the roof of your mouth and is lightly held in place by the front part of your tongue.

Next, try to force a steady stream of air from your gut over the call. It's not like whistling, but more like saying a long, drawn-out word like "chuck." Don't worry about what sounds you get. The important thing is that you get some sound from the call.

Practice until you can get a steady, unwavering note for a few seconds. Don't get discouraged if it takes some time. It will come. When you can, start using a little tongue pressure to get the high part of a yelp. After that's become easy, back your tongue off a little and the tone will change to the low part at the end of the yelp.

From there on you gradually shorten the sounds, making sure that you have the high and low on each call. It may help to keep repeating "chuck." The next thing you know you're yelping.

No matter what your spouse or friends say, there's no such thing as too much practice. Beginners ought to have the call in their mouths every day. Call while riding to and from work and any other times you can get away with it. You need to be able to call without really concentrating.

If you have a friend who's a good caller, try to mimic him. Invest in a good instructional tape and call along with it. Practice, practice, practice.

Once you've gotten some control over the call, start working on calling very softly as well as quickly and slowly. Practice making a single yelp and a string of up to thirty yelps.

After you've mastered the simple yelp, try getting some short clucks from the call. Simply popping your lips together can usually make the sounds of such short-note calls as putts.

Purring is a little more difficult, both to explain and to accomplish. Try to loosen your tongue on your call so that your tongue vibrates when you blow air through your mouth. Stick with it. It's the kind of thing that might elude you for weeks or months and then suddenly it will just start to work for you.

Taking a tape recorder to the woods is an excellent way to see how you sound. Tape your calls on the recorder; then back off about sixty yards to see how you'll sound to the turkeys.

Many hunters put their hands to their mouths for simple comfort while others do so to improve their sound. Putting a cupped hand to your mouth does more than just improve sound. I use my hand like a small megaphone to send calls in different directions. Most turkeys don't stand in one spot to do all of their calling; so I try to sound like a bird that's walking around.

Experienced and novice hunters alike need to remember that there's no such thing as being too good with a diaphragm call. Keep practicing and don't be afraid to try something different. Once you've mastered one call, try a more difficult one. Check the market from time to time and look for innovations.

Do some experimenting with a couple of new calls every year, and don't rule out trying different manufacturers. You never know when there might be something better out there.

Calling Devices

Spend as much time as possible listening to good turkey calling—from tapes, videos, at contests or from local experts. Ask someone for help if there's a call you're having problems with. There may be a short cut that could work well for you.

Like all instruments, diaphragm turkey calls require a little care to work their best. Keep the calls in their protective cases when they're not in your mouth, and never leave them near intense heat or in direct sunlight.

If your call is dry and your reeds are stuck together, don't start pulling and jerking. The reeds rip easily. Instead, wallow the call around in your mouth for a while and let it get good and wet. Calling may vibrate the reeds open. If it doesn't, try holding the call between your fingers and softly blowing some air to free the reeds.

Diaphragm calls will last longer if stored in a refrigerator or freezer when they're not in use. Carefully sliding flat toothpicks between the reeds is another little trick that can help protect the life of a call.

Placing flat toothpicks in a multiple-reed diaphragm call will help prolong its life and preserve a good tone. *Photo by Ray Eye.*

Voice

One advantage to calling with your vocal cords is that they're always with you. Your voice can also sound more natural than an artificial call. Additionally, turkeys don't often hear voice calls. There are times when call-shy turkeys will readily respond to the natural sounds of a good voice caller.

Looking back, I've probably called more turkeys with my bare voice than any other way, and I've taught a lot of hunters who now use voice calls regularly. With practice, most turkey hunters can master them.

As with all calls, the voice call is tough to explain on paper. Mouth yelping basically revolves around the word "calk." Start off saying the word regularly, then begin taking it up in pitch, gradually moving it to the back of your throat.

Don't force it. Having your throat and vocal cords relaxed is important. Give yourself plenty of time and stick with it. There's probably no bigger thrill in calling than using your natural voice to harvest a wild turkey.

Turkey hunters trying to take advantage of a spring tom's excited gobbling have several locating calls to choose from. Most are inexpensive and easy to use.

Owl Hooter

Even a small child can get owl hoots from one of the small, barrel-shaped owl hooters that are currently on the market. Many avid hunters take the time to learn how to make the notes of a barred owl using only their voices. It can be a lot of fun and very effective once you get the hang of it.

Crow Call

The crow call is probably the most universal of all locating calls. Coast to coast, turkeys readily respond to the shrill caws of a number of manufactured crow calls. The higher the pitch the better; keep the calls short and excited.

Other Calls

Hunters can also utilize the high squeal of hawk and predator calls, coyote howlers, and elk bugles. A tight triple-reed call can be used to make the high-pitched screams of the same calls.

6
Scouting

No matter where they're from, a few good turkey hunters always seem to tag a bird on opening morning. Over the years I've met many of these hunters, and they're all different. Some call like pros while others don't. Some carry a wide selection of new mouth calls, and some use a weathered old box call that's fooled hundreds of turkeys through many generations.

But there is one thing each of these never-fail hunters has in common—scouting. They know exactly where the turkeys are at any given time of any given day. That makes things much easier. No matter how good you are, you can't call turkeys if they aren't there.

Over the years many people have asked me when they should start scouting. A good turkey hunter actually scouts year-round.

I spend much of my summer, fall, and winter looking over new turkey country. I'm not looking for turkeys as much as I am good habitat. Experience will tell you what the turkeys in your home state prefer.

Look for a good stand of timber. Obviously that varies from region to region. For the Rio Grande hunter it may be as skimpy as a few cottonwoods along a dry creek or a long, towering evergreen shelterbelt. Such surroundings would rarely deserve a second look in good eastern country.

Finding water is one of the main considerations when checking out a new area. *Photo by Mike Pearce.*

Scouting

Good turkey habitat also needs adequate food and water. If you're planning to hunt the spring season you should look for plenty of good nesting habitat. Find a place with nesting hens in the spring and you'll find gobblers.

If you're new to the area, or if your state's still in a restocking program, you may want to make sure there are birds around before spending much time scouting. Local landowners and conservation agents are good sources of information, as are rural mail carriers and school bus drivers.

A lot of hunters, myself included, like to combine turkey scouting trips with fall hunting. The thousands of hours I've spent combing the woods for squirrels and whitetails have been a big help during turkey seasons.

The fall and winter is an excellent time to get to know the lay of the land. Look for barriers like creeks, fences, and steep bluffs. Find where game and logging trails begin and end.

Look for potential strutting areas and calling sights. It's a lot easier to get a feel for the land when the leaves are on the ground.

Learn the different ways you can approach an area. Finding the back door into a good piece of public property can give you a big advantage over the competition.

Of course you want to keep an eye out for the turkeys themselves, but don't be overly concerned if you don't see any on your winter scouting trips. In many regions turkeys travel to wintering areas where they may build flocks of several hundred birds.

Where these wintering birds congregate is usually common knowledge. You can ask conservation agents or local landowners if you don't already know. If possible, check in on the flock from time to time so you'll know when the birds begin to disperse in the spring.

In the meantime, get to know the property. The more time you can spend looking over the lay of the land when the season is still months away, the better. You'll want to devote the few weeks before opening day concentrating on finding and learning about individual birds.

When it looks as if spring is here to stay, it's time to start walking, looking, and listening. Look for tracks around the edges of fields, at creek crossings, along dirt roads—any place they might show in the soil. Naturally, gobbler tracks are going to be noticeably larger than hen tracks. But generally, where you find hens, you'll find gobblers when the mating season rolls around.

Droppings are another good indicator of an area's turkey population. Most people already know how to distinguish the J-shaped gobbler drop-

Spend some time looking over good turkey country. Here Ray is looking for ridges, open fields, and any natural obstructions that could keep a gobbler from coming to calls. *Photo by Tom Huggler.*

One good sign is a fresh track that's clearly visible in the soft dirt. Old trails, field edges, and creek crossings are good places to check for tracks. *Photo by Mike Pearce.*

pings from the round, popcorn-like ones of a hen. Keep your eyes open for feathers, scratchings, and dusting areas as well.

Hunters also need to realize that where they live determines what they're looking for when scouting. There are places in good Rio Grande habitat where you can walk all day and not see any scratchings. But if you look closely, you might notice that most of the cow pies have been overturned—by turkeys pecking the bugs and worms from beneath. I've seen the same thing in eastern habitat as well.

Relying strictly on droppings can be misleading when hunting mountain Merriams. Due to low humidity and the make-up of their diet, what the turkeys pass may not disintegrate for days.

Your ears can help you cover a lot of ground even if the toms aren't gobbling much. A few good fall calls can often get an old hen or gobbler yelping. You can also listen for wingbeats and roost talk at first and last light.

In some areas a good pair of binoculars can help you find the birds. From a high point, check fields and meadows for birds feeding or sunning in the early morning or late afternoon.

Some of the freshest signs of all—moist turkey droppings. Hunters can tell a lot from droppings: the size of the bird, its gender, and what it has been feeding on. *Photo by Mike Pearce.*

Another good sign that a gobbler is in the area is a fresh black-tipped feather. *Photo by Mike Pearce.*

A turkey feeding in a field will pick up seeds, bugs, and grasshoppers. In the hardwoods turkeys will feed on the mast crop, such as acorns or seeds. To find turkeys in your hunting area it is very important to find the food sources they are using at that time of year. *Photo by Ray Eye.*

Visual siting of wild turkeys in your hunting area is the best turkey sign of all. *Photo by Ray Eye.*

Scouting

When the toms start gobbling, your scouting gets a whole lot easier, but it's as important as ever. I try to spend many mornings cruising the edges of my hunting grounds, listening for gobbles.

If you know an area well and hunt it often, sometimes you won't need to start scouting until the birds are gobbling. In good, unchanged habitat gobblers stay in the same general places from one season to the next.

Depending on where the birds are in their breeding cycle, you may be able to get responses to a locating call. It's also fairly safe to use a gobble now. Try to check as many spots as possible during that half-hour when birds are gobbling from the roost.

One of the biggest mistakes you can make is to bother birds so much that they change patterns. But with a little caution, you can learn much by exploring on foot a few days before the season opens.

Despite what some people say, I do quite a bit of calling a few weeks before the season. Some say it educates the birds. I say it educates the hunter, provided he doesn't overdo it by calling the bird in close and spooking it.

I can't count the times I've called to a certain bird every day for a week before the season. I'm not taking about pouring it on; I'd call just enough to get him to sound off once. But on opening morning I'd know right where he'd be. I would move in close and pour it on, and he'd run right to me.

If possible, I use a locating call at first light and move in close while the birds are still on the roost so that I can learn where they head when they fly down. No matter how well I know an area, I also take the time to check it one last time, looking for any changes.

A couple of days before the season is the time to check the meadows and clearings for strutting turkeys, breast feathers, or the marks made by dragging wingtips to see if an area is used for strutting. If you're lucky you'll find indications that a bird uses a spot day after day.

If you've done your job, you should know the general location of anywhere from six to sixty gobblers before the season opens. Strive to remember everything you've learned about each one of them.

Personally, I always carry a topographical map to chart the location of each gobbler I hear, making special note of high densities or a bird with easily discernable behavior patterns. If you make such a map, keep it hidden and guard it with your life. You may be able to trust your best friend or brother with your car, children, or deepest secret—but not with a piece of paper that shows the way to a quartet of toms that are gobbling their brains out all morning. (You could, of course, trust me.)

This photograph shows how strutting wears the wingtips on a gobbler. Hunters should look for the little drag marks they leave in soft soil. *Photo by Mike Pearce.*

Remember that you never really stop scouting, not even when the season begins. Keep your eyes open as you move through the woods. Things can change for better or worse from day to day.

Hunters who find themselves hunting unfamiliar territory can scout as they go. Cover as much ground as possible so you can learn the lay of the land and the ways of the turkeys. If you hear some gobbling or find some fresh sign, stop and work the area.

Keep your ears and eyes open for other hunters. Drive the roads in your hunting area and look for parked vehicles as you enter and leave to see if you have company. If so, you may want to either approach from another direction or perhaps even try another site.

Thanks to your good scouting, you'll know right where to go.

7

Spring Hunting

A new day begins early when you're a spring turkey hunter, often at a time many people would still characterize as "last night." Farm houses lie as dark as they would in a power outage, and highways that will later be dotted with commuters are open and desolate.

The woods at your destination may be rolling seas of hardwoods or thin ribbons of cottonwoods. Either way, they are full of invitation as you enter in the predawn grayness.

It's almost magical, this time of indecision between night and day. Your senses are on full alert as you walk a familiar trail. Even in the gloom your eyes pick up the ivory blossoms of a budding dogwood or sand plum; your nostrils become alive with their sweet fragrance. The dew-laden grasses feel cool and wet as they brush against your legs.

But it's your ears and what they hear that demand your full attention. As the increasing light spreads across the eastern horizon, so do the sounds of the new day. First comes the occasional chirp of a songbird or maybe the raspy call of a cock pheasant.

By the time you reach your stopping place the woods are in full chorus. Songbirds flit about while the mournful sounds of a great horned owl roll across the land.

Yet you wait for the one sound that has been on your mind for months—the rattling gobble of a turkey. You needn't look at your watch to know it could erupt at any second. The brightening woods and your quickening pulse tell you it's gobbling time.

It is without a doubt the most exciting time of the day. It's also the time of the most uncertainty. Will there be any gobbling to be heard? Where will it come from? Will you be able to get there in time to work the bird while he's still on the limb?

You can rest a little more comfortably if you've scouted before the season. Success is almost a sure thing if you scouted the woods the night before.

A good Missouri eastern comes to calls first thing in the morning. A hunter who's put a bird to bed the night before has an excellent chance of moving in close before daylight and bringing a roosted bird into gun range after flydown. *Ron Godi, Jr.*

This tom makes positive identification easy. Note the black-tipped breast feathers, the red and blue head, and most importantly the visible beard. *Ray Eye*

Above: The back view of a turkey in full strut. Since his vision is blocked, now is an excellent time to raise a gun. Make sure his head is raised before you fire; a simple "putt" will do the trick.

This turkey is Eugene, featured in chapter twenty-five. Though Ray had him in range many times, he was never able to bag him. Notice the size of his spurs—he was an old and dominant gobbler. *Ray Eye*

Right: Who says you can't call fall gobblers. Ray called in this late-October tom to within a few yards using gobbler yelps and cutting. *Ray Eye*

Opposite: The combination of a camouflaged hunter and a camouflaged gun let the hunter get within a few steps of this eastern. *Mike Pearce*

It's possible to get a little too hidden. Hunters need to make sure the turkey can't see them, but they also need enough room to shoot when the time comes. Ray usually likes to sit with his back against a big tree. But with more and more needless hunting accidents happening in the woods, some hunters may resort to such drastic measures as these for safety. *Ray Eye*

A longbeard coming to calls. When the weather is off and the birds are not responding to mating calls, Ray will use gobbler yelps to call a tom into range. *Ray Eye*

This big gobbler is strutting his stuff to calls along a hardwood ridgetop. As tempting as it may be, don't even think about pulling the trigger before the bird raises his head and neck. *Ron Godi, Jr.*

See how this strutting tom lifts his feathers and drops his wings. If a hunter listens closely, he'll probably hear the sounds of the tom strutting and drumming. *Jeff Murray*

Opposite: When not in the depths of passion, such as in the fall or late spring, mature gobblers hang together in the woods like these two nice toms. *Ray Eye*

The hunter has accomplished the hard part of getting his bow drawn. Now he has to wait for a perfectly clear shot. A shot at either of these birds is too risky because the arrow might be deflected by a small branch. One good shot is better than a dozen uncertain ones; and there's no bird worth risking a crippling shot. *Ray Eye*

Below: Oops! In about half a second there's going to be one running turkey. The tom has seen the photographer and has probably already started putting. Sometimes the hunter can putt right back and stop the bird long enough for a shot. *Ray Eye*

8

Roosting

Roosting, or as some call it "putting a bird to bed," is basically waiting in the woods at dusk and listening for a gobbler to betray his location. Once he's discovered, you know exactly where to begin the next morning's hunt. If all goes well you can sneak in close and work the gobbler on the roost when he's probably the most vulnerable to calling.

In the right situation, roosting can be a very effective tactic. In fact, I owe one of the biggest birds of my hunting career, at least in part, to roosting.

Dusk was still more than an hour away as I made my way across a long Ozark ridge that was intersected by a series of smaller adjoining ridges. It was the day before the opener (the longest day of the year for a turkey hunter), and I was on the ridge by choice. My pre-season scouting had revealed that there were several toms in the area. One big old bird was the unmistakable boss.

Moving as quietly as possible, I sat down in a place where I could hear down several of the small ridges and waited. The shadows of sunset extended almost from horizon to horizon when the bird's first gobble split the silence.

Many hunters would have been content just to know the bird's general location, but the more precisely you can pinpoint a bird the better. He sounded about three hundred yards away. I started a slow, quiet stalk toward his roost, stopping occasionally to give a soft great horned owl hoot to get him to gobble.

I stopped about eighty yards short of the bird, taking a seat beside an old oak that was at about the same level as the gobbler and near the edge of an old logging road. Egged on by my hoots and the natural sounds of the forest, the old bird was still hammering out gobbles when I crept from the moonlit hillside.

It was hard not to be confident. I can't prove the theory, but it seems as if birds that are fired up in the evening are usually in the same frame of mind the next morning.

With my strategy already planned, I quietly sneaked back to the old oak long before daylight. With the first signs of light and sounds of songbirds, I gave a few soft tree yelps. There was no gobble, but the sound of the tom drumming on a limb told me we were still in business.

A little later I hit him with a few yelps. He answered with a long chorus of gobbles. He gobbled at almost everything: other turkeys gobbling in the distance, crows, owls, and sometimes at nothing at all.

With fly-down time at hand, I was afraid his nonstop gobbling might attract some camouflaged attention. So I opened up with a series of fast cackles like a hen flying down from a limb. After pausing a few seconds I came back with some soft, soothing purrs—like a hen content to move around on the ground.

The big tom flew down and triple-gobbled on the old logging road about fifty yards to my right. Again, I sent him some aggressive cutting which brought him in at a fast trot, slowing only to gobble and break into a half-strut. I was back in camp by 6 A.M.

The tom was large for a mountain bird: 23½ pounds, with an 11½-inch beard and, even more impressively, 1½-inch spurs.

It's too bad all roosting episodes don't end with such ease and happiness. Roosting turkeys vary a lot. For one thing, the birds have to be in good gobbling cycles. Hit them too early or too late in the breeding season and there will be little, if any, limb talk.

There can also be a great deal of variety across the country. In my home state of Missouri it's getting tougher to get even a single evening gobble, but I've had as many as eight or ten different Merriams responding well to calls long after dark in South Dakota's Black Hills.

Again, I think that hunting pressure has more to do with it than breeding. Throughout the early 1970s, I can remember being in the only camp in a section of national forest in Missouri, listening to turkeys gobbling all around us as we ate supper. That same ground now has about as many hunters as trees, and it's tough to get a bird to gobble in the morning, let alone the evening.

But if you have the time, and the birds are right, roosting can definitely be worth the effort. Try and get into the woods an hour before dark. Go where you know there are turkeys, but try to get away from the commotion of roads or running water. If possible, stick to the high country where you can hear more territory.

One of the main objectives is not to disturb the surroundings and the turkeys. Spend more time listening than calling and keep your ears open for hen talk, gobbling, and wingbeats of birds flying up to roost.

Most hunters wisely opt for natural locating calls, such as owl hoots, crow calls, or coyote howls. Try to use what the birds might have been gobbling at for days. If you're hunting eastern turkeys, that might be barred owl hoots. If Rios are your birds, try crow or coyote calls.

And don't limit yourself to one call. Just because they aren't gobbling at one doesn't mean that they won't go nuts over another. I once used a shrill crow call and got but a single Merriam gobble, but seconds later a high-pitched coyote howl from a diaphragm call brought seven different responses. The next night the gobblers' reactions could have been just the opposite. Don't try to figure them out; just be prepared to try anything.

And that anything should include hen calls. Sure, you don't hear much about them, but that doesn't mean they won't work. For one thing, soft talk may get a response from some otherwise silent hens.

There are also times during the breeding season when gobblers don't seem to gobble at anything but hen calls. The first time I hunted Massachusetts with Gerry Bethge of *Outdoor Life*, I could crow or owl until my lungs ached and not get a gobble. When I opened up with some aggressive hen calls on a box call, though, I couldn't get the turkeys to shut up.

As with any calling, hens calls should start off softly with a few clucks and yelps, gradually building in volume and intensity to excited cutting and cackling at fly-up time.

There are several theories on the best way to venture into the woods at roosting time. Most hunters like to separate and spread out to cover as much ground as possible. If one hunter hears several different birds, everybody in camp might have a gobbler to work at dawn.

But John Hauer likes to use the buddy system when guiding hunters in the Black Hills. Hauer, who can move faster than a white-tailed deer through rock and pine country, likes his hunters in one spot blowing a locating call to keep a bird gobbling while he sneaks in close. Come morning, he often knows the exact tree in which the turkey sits and his calling sight is already chosen and free of debris. That bird usually doesn't live to gobble from another roost.

But there are several other items to keep in mind when it comes to roosting turkeys. One is other hunters. Get a gobbler to respond eight or ten times in an evening on crowded public ground and the closest road may look like a used-car lot the next morning.

Additionally, the evening's events may have nothing to do with those of the morning. You can go into an area in the evening and hear nothing, but at dawn you'll hear four or five gobblers.

On a positive side, it's often the most dominant birds that do the roost gobbling. Finding a good gobbling bird in the evening may mean working a bird with golf tee-sized spurs the next morning.

And not everyone has the time or desire to go out and roost birds. Personally, I seldom roost birds on my home hunting grounds in Missouri for the simple reason that my scouting has already shown me where the birds are.

Granted, hearing a bird sound off from his perch is a big help, but that doesn't mean you're out of luck come morning. No, if you play your cards right you can still have a heck of a duel on your hands with the coming of dawn.

9

Duel at Dawn

There is no time between daylight and dark that can compare with those magical minutes when the turkeys are just awakening on the roosts. Some days you can hear more gobbling in these twenty minutes than in the next ten hours. This is also the time when your chances for success are best, especially when the hunting is tough. You don't want to miss even a minute of it.

Consequently, it's far better to be a little early than a little late. I like to be at my listening post at least twenty minutes before gobbling time. Of course it's best to be in the place your scouting has shown to be populated with the most birds, or in an area with several birds and no other hunters.

Again, if you're in rolling country, try to stick to high ground, such as a main ridge. That way you can hear well, and you're also in a central location to move toward gobbling birds. You can also cover more ground more quickly if one area proves disappointing.

If the birds are gobbling well you won't need to worry about a locating call. But if it's getting light and the other birds are in full voice, you may want to try an owl hoot or crow calls. If they don't work then try some hen talk.

Again, start off softly. Every day of the season some hunter gives a

Stick to the high country until a bird responds. This principle is the same nationwide. *Photo by Mike Pearce.*

hoot at the top of his lungs and scares a tom that was just waking up a short distance down the ridge.

Also, don't make your locating calls too complex. If a bird is really fired up, he may answer so quickly that your own noise keeps you from hearing him. Get loud and aggressive only when the soft and short calls aren't working.

If fly-down time is rapidly approaching and you still haven't heard a bird, you may want to consider either moving on or perhaps heading to a different area. Just because the birds aren't gobbling doesn't mean they aren't there, but in most cases the more a bird gobbles on the roost the more apt he is to respond to your calls when he's on the ground.

But let's say that everything goes well instead. You get to your chosen spot, light is just beginning to spread through the trees, and it happens—a bird gobbles. Seconds later you hoot and he double-gobbles a reply. What you do next depends a lot on how far away the bird is and what the gobbling has been like on past mornings.

If you've been on this same ridge for three days straight and he's the first bird you've heard, then you probably shouldn't waste any time getting to him. But, if you know there are many birds in the area and that first gobble comes from way off, you may want to wait a few minutes to see what happens.

It's tough to hold back, but a little patience may well be rewarded. As sure as you make a beeline for that first gobble in the predawn, you'll walk right out and spook a bird that was even closer. You'll probably do this at least once in your turkey hunting career. And when you do you'll feel just as stupid as I do when I spook a bird that was only one hundred yards away to chase one that was five times as far off.

You also don't want to rush off without some kind of game plan in mind. Spend a few moments trying to picture the terrain near the bird's location. If you don't know exactly where the bird is, look for barriers like swamps and rivers while you're still in a position to avoid them.

Unless the bird is really close you'll want to move closer. How close? It's a question of feet, but I like to get absolutely as close as possible. The farther you have to call a bird, the more that can go wrong. The longer he's on the ground, the greater the chance a real hen will make an interception.

The same thing goes for other hunters, both two- and four-legged. On my last Rio Grande hunt we had a heck of a problem with coyotes setting up between us and the birds we were working. We practically had to set up in a turkey's lap to get him in before the coyotes came.

One of the biggest and most frequent mistakes made by hunters is heading directly at a gobbling bird. It's the shortest route but it's also a good way to spook a turkey.

I like to circle around before coming in on a gobbling bird for a number of reasons. One is that you can never be totally sure how close a gobbler is. He may sound three hundred yards away simply because he's gobbling in a hollow or facing away from you on the roost. If so, you could easily stumble upon him when you think you have room to spare. Another problem can occur when you use hen calls: the bird can fly down and head right toward you.

But you can still be in good shape if your approach cuts an arch. Even if you've overrun the bird's roost all you have to do is circle back and you're in business.

Another often overlooked mistake when moving and setting up on a turkey is getting sky-lighted along a hill or ridgetop. It may seem dark, but there will almost always be enough light for a gobbler to see you against the sky. Try to keep a ridge between you and the gobbler's location.

There's no way I can tell you exactly how close to get. I've actually moved in as close as forty yards, but other times open woods have forced me to stay as far as two hundred yards back. It all depends on the terrain

Never sky-light or silhouette yourself in a calling position or on an approach to a gobbler. *Photo by Ray Eye.*

and your chances of slipping in without spooking the bird. If you're the kind of hunter who makes a lot of noise when he's walking, then just accept that fact and hang a little farther back. The same rule holds if the woods are as open as a city park.

But ideally, I like to set up within seventy-five to one hundred yards of a roosted bird. It's just as important, though, to be on the right side of the bird.

Whenever I'm moving toward a bird on the roost I try to figure out in which direction he would naturally head. Sometimes it's a simple process of elimination; the birds won't usually fly down into thick brush or onto really steep hillsides.

Ideally, it's best to be set up on the same level as the gobbler, or maybe a little higher. Try to pick a route that will make it easy for the bird to get to you — no fences, thick brambles, or standing water. If you can set up along a natural travel lane like an old logging road or game trail, so much the better.

Sometimes, if you pay attention, the turkeys can let you know the best side to set up for a roosted gobbler. If you hear the tom answering the calls of hens or other toms farther away it might be best to set up between the two groups.

Also think back to how the birds have been reacting over the past few days. Awareness of even a vague pattern can work to your benefit.

In 1987, *Fishing & Hunting Journal* editor Ron Kruger and I were in southern Kansas for the opening day of the first season that allowed nonresident turkey hunters. A friend had gotten us permission to hunt near an abandoned farm. He claimed that the birds usually roosted north of the old home, then fed in the nearby area.

We sounded a crow call near the old place and a bird immediately answered. But he and the rest of a flock were roosting in some trees several hundred yards south of the house, not north as our friend had claimed. Figuring the birds would want to stay in the same area to feed, we set up between the house and the birds.

We were right. One particular gobbler was cutting all of my calls and came strutting to within twenty steps — where Ron took him the minute the season opened. Had we set up on one of the other sides of the house, the bird may not have come in or may have come a little more slowly. I'll never know, because given a choice I'll call from the place where the bird already wants to go.

10
After Flydown

There are times—many, many times—when the classic hunt of working a bird on a limb doesn't unfold as it should. It's disappointing, but it's far from the end of a hunt. It simply means you find a bird with both feet on the ground that is willing to use them to come to you.

Sometimes you can spend a little extra time on a bird that's gobbled to you on the roost, but hasn't come in, and eventually take him. But if you can't, or the bird simply quits gobbling, it's probably time to find a bird that's still talking. Just because one bird won't cooperate doesn't mean you can't find another that will charge right in like a kamikaze.

Spend a few seconds recalling where you've heard other gobblers that morning or the previous evening within the immediate area. If there isn't any gobbling it may be time to change to a new area, giving the birds you're working on a few hours' rest.

Again, I stick to the high country when trying to locate a bird on the ground. If the bird is in the right state of mind I use the same locating calls that I do in the morning or evening—especially the owl hoots and crow calls.

If the birds have been gobbling well at all, I try to cover a lot of ground. How far I travel between calling sights depends on terrain, weather, and my confidence in the immediate area. In Missouri, I usually

Turkeys are amazingly good flyers, though they prefer to run. *Photo by Mike Blair.*

only go about two hundred yards before giving the birds another call. If it's windy I may cut the distance in half, but if it's dead calm and I'm on a real high ridge I may double it.

When using locating calls you don't really have to spend a lot of time in one place. If a gobbler is going to respond to a hoot or crow call, he'll usually do it after a series or two.

But sometimes the birds don't respond to locating calls. How they react on and off the roost tells you whether you'll need to use turkey calls for locating gobblers. Generally, if there's little limb talk, you can hang up the hoots and crow calls. It's time to talk one-on-one.

But first you should realize the problems of using turkey talk when you're moving and calling. One is that the bird may run right in before you get a chance to set up. The second is the element of danger. No matter how much hunters preach safety and positive identification there are still people out there who stalk turkey calls and shoot at sounds and/or movement.

It usually pays to do a quick set-up when you're moving and hen calling. After you've let the woods settle a little, make a few soft yelps or clucks to break the ice. If nothing gobbles, start building both intensity and volume.

Different terrains offer different challenges. In the open country of Rio Grandes, simply getting from one calling spot to another without being seen can be tough. This smart hunter uses a dry creek bottom to hide his approach. *Photo by Mike Pearce.*

Don't make the mistake of using only one or two standard calls. If the birds are really quiet it may take some excitement or a loud and high-pitched box call to get them going.

And this is a prime case where good calling—like real excited cutting and gobbler yelps—can make the difference between silence and gobbling. During the 1988 spring season in Missouri (and in most states I hunted that year), long and lively cutting was the only call the birds responded to consistently.

But no matter what the reason, suppose you just got a bird to gobble at one of your calls. Now what? Do you hold your ground, back up, move forward, lie down, stand up . . . ?

Again, each situation is unique. You have to evaluate the terrain between you and the bird: how far he is, where he is, where he's going, what's between you and him, and whether he gets to you easily and quickly.

If the responding gobbler sounds as if he's so close he's within gun range—and on rare occasions this happens—I hold my ground and don't move a muscle.

If he sounds as if he's within one hundred yards I may try to bring him on in. But otherwise I seldom try to work a bird without getting closer to him. Working a bird long-distance is only asking for trouble in the form of hens, other hunters, or any number of interruptions. The shorter the distance, the fewer possible problems.

Additionally, moving toward the bird, even by only thirty or forty yards, adds a great deal of realism to your calling. You sound like a hen that's really looking for a gobbler. If he thinks you're moving in his general direction he may get excited enough to come meet you.

As with a bird on the roost, gobbling turkeys should never be approached head on. Try to figure out the path the bird will probably take as he's moving in your direction. If you're on one ridge and he gobbles from another, you may want to hustle over and set up in the saddle where the two ridges meet.

On the other hand, if you're on a fairly steep ridge and the bird gobbles from a meadow below, you may have to cut around and work him from the same level. Whatever you do, make it as easy as possible for the bird to come to you.

Don't waste a lot of time, but don't be in a big hurry either. Your next move—choosing a good calling position—is one of the most important. It's also the key mistake made by many hunters.

11
Calling Positions

O.K., let's say the bird gobbled at an obnoxious string of crow calls and you have his position well pinpointed. You've chosen what you feel is the easiest, most natural route for him to take.

Now you want to find a calling position that will do you the most good. Sure, it's tempting to set up where you can watch the bird coming for a long way. But remember that the more you can see of a gobbler the better his chances of either seeing you or figuring out that something isn't right.

Whenever possible, I like to set up so that I can't see the gobbler (and vice versa) until he's within killing range. I've always liked a little break in the hill between us—or maybe a sharp bend in a tree line or logging road.

It's best if the vegetation is thick enough to block the bird's view but not his progress. You want him to be able to move without fear of being ambushed by predators, yet blinded enough that he's lured on by the hen that is just out of sight.

Most of the time calling from a sitting position is best. It puts you at about eye level with the turkey and usually offers a reasonable field of view.

Try to find a tree that's at least as wide as your shoulders to shield

It is essential to have a calling position that makes it easy for the turkey to come to you and for you to make a clean kill. *Photo by Ray Eye.*

Do not choose a calling position where the surrounding area is too thick with vegetation. You do not want the gobbler to get in too close, as in this photo. A good set-up would have an open area in front of the hunter so that when the gobbler appears he is within twenty-five to thirty yards. *Photo by Ray Eye.*

your outline. Take a few seconds to clear away anything that might interfere with your gun movement or become uncomfortable to sit on for any amount of time.

Remember that you don't have to tunnel into the ground or shield yourself with a lot of cover. One of my biggest, and now funniest, mistakes was trying to set up inside a dense bunch of brambles when I was a kid. Sure, the bird couldn't see me but I also couldn't see him when he walked within twenty yards. I almost never got free of all those vines and thorns.

Personally, I like to sit in a kind of laid back slouch, so that I'm low to the ground and able to keep my gun resting on my raised knees.

There are times when it's best not to call from a sitting position. Sometimes all you can do is hold your ground and pray for the best.

My dad and I managed a slow hunt on a rainy morning a few years ago. Our plan was for me to cover some ground, find a bird we could work, and then go back to get Dad so that we could set up on the bird together.

Well, events don't always unfold as planned. I heard a tom and some hens in a patch of woods near some overgrown farm fields. I circled around the open fields hoping to get a better feel for the area and the location of the birds.

A good set-up on a Missouri hardwood ridgetop. Both hunters have their backs against trees that are wider than their shoulders. *Photo by Mike Pearce.*

As a gobbler approaches your calling position, never move anything if you can see his head. Look for an opening for your shot. Tree limbs and ground cover will deflect a lot of shots and the result can be a crippled bird. *Photo by Ray Eye.*

Even though I knew better, and even though I preach the contrary, I stopped while I was still essentially out in the open, behind a small tree, and gave a few cuts. The hens cut my calls and popped into view, coming over a slight rise. There I was, with nothing but an eight-inch tree between me and them.

Luckily for me, the hens were so excited that they never stopped running. When the gobbler followed them I took him with a faceful of No. 6 shot. I felt like a kid with his hand in a cookie jar when Dad came up and asked who was supposed to be calling and who was supposed to be shooting.

And across much of America's turkey country there simply isn't enough underbrush to conceal a hunter sitting in front of a tree. The ponderosa pine country of the Merriams and the cottonwood tree lines of the Rios are prime examples. It's sometimes the same with easterns.

Back in 1987 I started a Massachusetts bird with an owl hoot, closed the distance, and hit him with a hen call. He gobbled right back. I circled about two hundred yards around him, but no matter where I went the woods were as open as a city park. You couldn't hide a squirrel, let alone a two hundred-pound hunter.

Whenever I'm faced with that scenario I use what I call a blocker tree. I got on my knees behind a big hemlock, my gun pointing up. I hardly peeked around the tree.

The bird was coming in from left to right, and a couple of times I had to ease left to keep from being seen. The main problem was that there just wasn't enough cover between me and the bird for me to shoulder the gun without being seen.

After what seemed like an eternity the bird stopped behind another tree twenty-five yards away. When he stepped out I took all twenty-one pounds of him. When I stood up, I realized I had unknowingly scooted all the way around to the opposite side of the tree.

Other times you can set up against a tree knowing full well that the gobbler is going to come in behind you. In those cases, direct your calls out in front of you, then let the turkey walk right into your field of fire as he looks for the hen he thinks is still before him.

I've even killed several birds from a standing position. To do so, flatten your body against the tree as if you were a long lump in the

If you're set up and calling and turkeys come into view but you cannot move your gun, sit perfectly still. Let the turkeys walk away, then reposition yourself and call them back in. *Photo by Ray Eye.*

These turkeys are approaching the hunter's calling position along the edge of a field. He made it easy for the turkeys to come to his location by using the lay of the land. *Photo by Ray Eye.*

Ray sets up with his back against a big tree and his gun resting on a raised knee and pointing in the direction of the responding gobbler. *Photo by Mike Pearce.*

bark; don't move until the right moment. Sometimes you can even find a tree whose branches fork at just the right height to accommodate a pointed gun.

Down in the hills where I learned much of what I know, mostly by a little trial and a lot of error, there was an open rock glade where, sitting at the edge, you couldn't see twenty yards. But there was a Y-shaped tree growing right in front of a massive old oak that made a perfect blind. We killed a lot of turkeys looking through the branches of that old tree.

But again, calling from a sitting position in front of a tree is best. Try other postures only as last resorts.

Don't make the mistake of sitting or standing in direct sunlight. Try to find a shadow. If possible the sun should be at your back to further limit the gobbler's ability to see you.

It's a very good idea to look around and pick a landmark or two at the edge of your gun range while you're still standing. Sitting can greatly reduce your depth perception; a turkey that's twenty yards away may sometimes look as if he's twice as far off—or vice versa.

If you're right-handed, try to sit with your left shoulder pointing in the direction of the bird's approach so that you'll have a full 180-degree field of fire. Naturally, if you're left-handed you want your right side facing the bird for the best shooting.

12
Strutting Areas

There is a place in the east-central Missouri Ozarks where a small rocky stream winds its way past a little glade. It's met by a sloping ridge and bordered by the remnants of an ancient split rail fence. At one end, not far from the little meadow's crown, sits a mammoth oak that seems as old as the hills themselves.

Rest your back against the old tree and face the small field of spring wildflowers and growing grass and you're in one of the finest places in America to call and take a wild turkey. I know, because I've done it eight or nine times myself. From the stories I've heard, my grandfather also did it numerous times when he was a young man in the hills.

Several hundred miles to the west in the red dirt country of western Oklahoma there is a clearing that is lined by a steep canyon on one side and a scattering of brush and junipers on the other.

This place, too, is an excellent one for taking a spring tom. My friend Milton Rose has been visiting this special place to fill the tags of his guided clients for years. Chances are, his young son will do the same throughout his life.

Both of these secluded little spots—the one in the timbered Ozarks and the other on the prairies of Oklahoma—are productive for the same reason: they're strutting areas.

It's only been within the past few years that the term "strutting area" has popped into turkey hunting parlance. Actually, good turkey hunters have known about these little open pockets for generations. For me, they were just certain glades in the Ozarks where the toms came to display and gobble. For others, they might be corners of green wheatfields or flat expanses of dry land in swampy country.

No matter where, the turkeys are using them for the same basic reasons. It's not as complex or mystifying as some people would have you believe. It's simply a good place for turkeys — especially the hens.

Most strutting areas are near good nesting cover for the hens and close to greens and bugs for food. Simple biology tells you that where you find hens during breeding season you also find toms, gobbling and displaying where they can be easily heard and seen.

But as with all spring hunting, working the strutting areas usually only succeeds during certain times of the breeding season. True, some toms will occasionally use a strutting area when trying to attract hens, but the best time to hunt the areas is when the mating season is either at its peak or starting its decline.

But it's never a matter of simply finding a small meadow or glade, making a few calls, then rolling a big longbeard when he runs up. There's the ever important right time and right place to be considered first.

You probably already know what it's going to take to find such a place: scouting. Look for the usual signs of fresh tracks and droppings that seem to appear in the same location day after day. Also keep an eye out for the little ditches in the soft dirt or leaves that are left by the wingtips of a strutting turkey.

In some areas it's even possible to get high on a ridge and survey the surrounding countryside for strutting gobblers. Hunters with access to a good topographical map can look for the appropriate open fields close to water and good nesting cover.

It's also possible to save a lot of walking time by scouting with your ears. If you or a friend has been working a bird that refuses to budge or that even heads in the opposite direction, there's a fair chance that he may be set up on a strutting area.

When you find yourself in such a situation, don't rush right after the gobbler. Take your time and get to know the terrain, even if it means waiting until later in the day. Move slowly and spend a lot of time looking and listening.

Several seasons ago I met a friend who was complaining about a bird he'd been working for several days. It was the same old story: "he'll gobble at all of my calls yet he always goes the other way."

Approaching the area with the hunter I found the perfect explana-

A hunter checks an open meadow for strutting or feeding turkeys. If he sees the birds he'll circle around, set up as close as possible, and start calling. *Photo by Mike Pearce.*

tion. The tom was simply leaving the roost and heading to an old clearing where a few old hog houses sat above a nice little creek. It had all of the requirements of a good strutting area—water, good cover for nesting hens, and a high location where the gobbler could see and be seen.

We slipped into the little meadow the next morning, the hunter took a seat at the meadow's edge, and I had no problems at all calling the bird right up to him, where he took it. The bird that had frustrated him for days was one of his easiest kills once we set up on the gobbler's strutting area.

As mentioned earlier, such hotspots can be tough to find, but they're more than worth the effort. As long as there are no major changes in habitat they'll produce from year to year, decade to decade.

Just as important, though, they'll often produce day after day when one gobbler steps in to take another's place. Our guided hunters ended up taking four more longbeards off the strutting area with the old hog barns during the remaining ten days of the Missouri season.

I also watched another friend pull a miracle miss. It simply must have been an act of God: he didn't kill a huge gobbler that was standing in the open with his head periscoped up less than twenty yards away.

How and when during the day you hunt strutting areas will depend a lot on where the turkeys are in their breeding cycles and how each individual tom is acting. Many times the tom will follow the hens wherever they go in the morning. Once they're on the nest the tom prowls other strutting areas looking for new loves.

Many times I've seen the birds roosting right at the edge of a strutting area, then using the glade for the first hour or two of daylight. In this situation the key is to move in as close as the terrain will allow before daylight, then call the bird from the roost. Even an old gobbler with four beauties on each side of him can get greedy enough to fly down a little early for some early action.

And there are also times when an area that seems devoid of turkeys early in the day will hold a strutting and gobbling tom at 10 or 11 A.M. Pay careful attention to when the birds use their strutting areas and from what direction they usually approach. Sometimes their schedules are like clockwork; and the more predictable the turkey, the easier it is to call him.

Also keep in mind that strutting areas are excellent places to try blind calling if the birds aren't gobbling. Some days even the dominant bird won't sound off even though he's strutting nearby. There's also a good chance that a sub-dominant bird is hanging around the area, hoping to steal a hen from the patriarch. These birds often sneak in quietly, literally looking over their shoulders for the whipping that they fear. Still, they don't want to leave the promise of a good strutting area.

The easiest way to take a turkey in a strutting area is to be there waiting for him when he appears. Chances are, if he's alone and already on the move, a little good calling can pull him right into your lap. Again, knowing the terrain and the patterns of the birds within it will tell you the time and place for calling.

Always remember to be careful when approaching a strutting area. One reason the birds like these areas so much is that they can see not only hens, but also predators. Use the terrain to block your approach and take some time to study the field for turkeys with each step.

Taking a bird that's already set up can be a real challenge. If the bird has hens feeding around him he probably won't want to leave them. When such is the case forget about the tom and start working on the hens.

Try to get the dominant hen fired up with aggressive cutting and yelps. Once she opens up, really pour it on. If she comes, the flock will probably follow, including the strutting gobbler.

Sometimes you can figure out a way to split the tom from the hens and then set up to call the old bird right in. I only use such a tactic as a last resort. It's usually better to study the birds and either wait until the

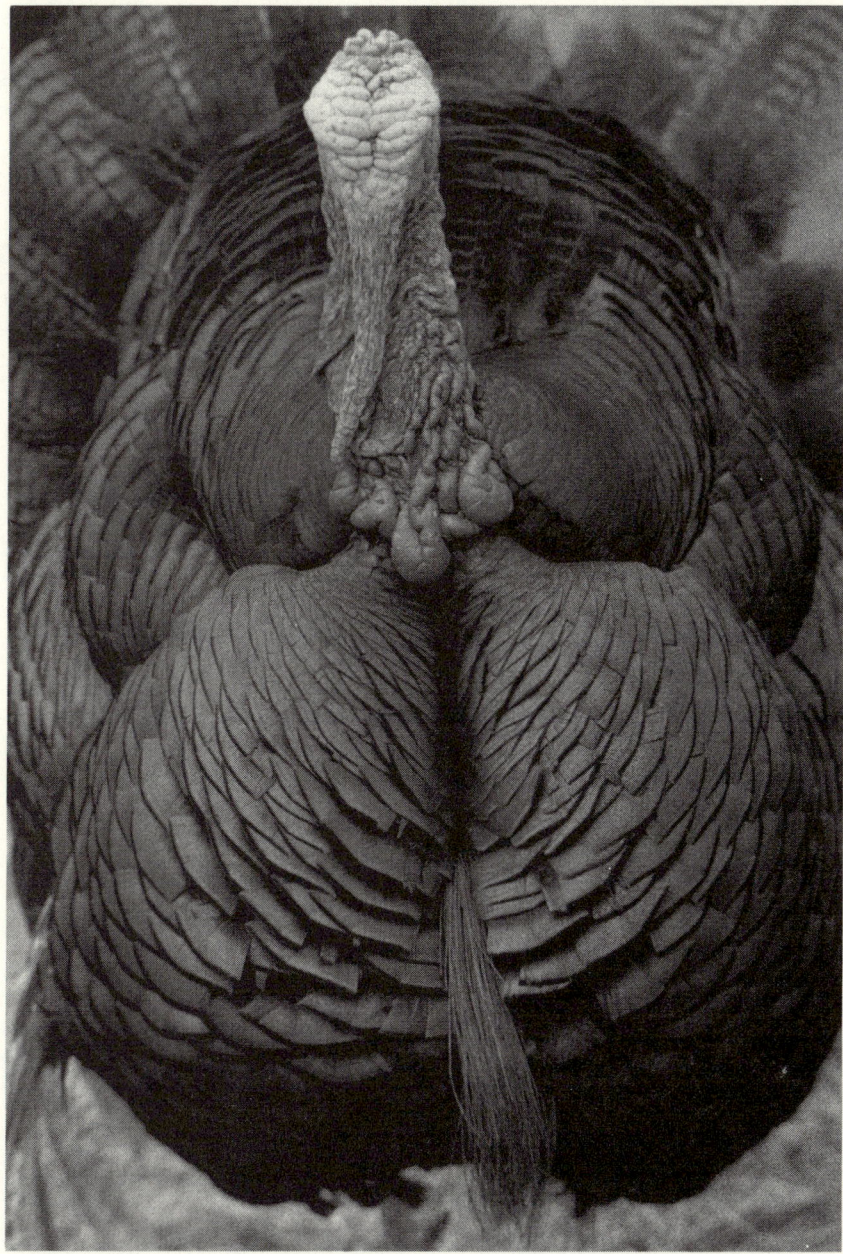

An eastern wild turkey gobbler in full strut. A strutting area can be used year after year if the terrain doesn't change. This is where you can hear the spit and drum of a strutting wild turkey: a deep hum that resembles a distant truck mired in the mud. *Photo by Ray Eye.*

hens leave or come back earlier the next morning, changing your calling position to the place where the tom and hens were strutting.

It can also be awfully difficult to pull a lone gobbler from the middle of a strutting area to a place where you can shoot him. If a gobbler is in a position where he can see well he may wait until the hen shows herself.

Sometimes you can hide behind a slight rise in elevation to fool the gobbler into thinking there's a hen just out of sight. Other times you can either turn and send your calls over your shoulder or ask your buddy to walk off calling like a hen playing hard to get.

And never forget the aggressive calls, such as excited hen calls and hard gobbler yelping and cutting. Get a big gobbler, or any other turkey that's in the area, fired up near a strutting area and you may see the show of your life.

A few days after I found the strutting area near the hog barn, Butch Milne and I were stood up by hunters we were supposed to guide. Not wanting to let a good morning go to waste we headed into the woods just as day was breaking.

Butch set out toward a gobble from the northwest while I headed in the general location of the strutting area. I didn't need to hoot to get the birds to gobble; they were cutting loose on their own. From the sounds of things they were still on the roost.

The spreading light meant that I couldn't move in and set up as usual; so I stayed back a little and tried to plan an approach that would get me close to the birds' roost. Using a ring of cedars for cover, I moved toward where the birds were talking.

By then it was so light that some of the hens were flying down, and the gobbler in the tree was gobbling at everything—owl hoots, crows, barking squirrels, hen calls, and especially the gobbles of another tom in a valley to the east.

I somehow managed to worm my way close to the roost tree without being seen. I made a soft call and the tom went crazy as several more hens pitched out of the tree and landed just a few feet from where I sat.

I figured the big bird would follow the ladies and the hunt would be over in a matter of seconds—but that wasn't the case. The gobbler sailed down but headed toward the other tom at a dead run, sending challenging gobbles with almost every step.

All I could do was sit there, as motionless as a camouflaged stump while I listened to the excited hen talk and the loud noises of two toms fighting it out eighty yards away.

When the fight was over the hens set out across a shallow, gravel-bottomed creek in single file, moving like one long, feathered snake up a winding trail toward the old pig barns. They passed so close I could hear their low putts and the soft sounds of their feet on the damp leaves.

Strutting Areas

The gobbler didn't respond to my soft calling; so I hurried north to set up where I knew the birds were headed. Easing up to the edge of the strutting area I couldn't see any turkeys. I crawled to some rocks and small cedars and looked again. This time I could see him in full strut, surrounded by hens at the other end of the glade sixty yards away.

Staying low, I gave a few soft hen calls. A couple of hens yelped back. The birds were at that awkward distance that's out of range yet too close to call loudly or move an inch. I buried my face in my chest and tried some fighting purrs and putts. Hens started racing back and forth and the tom slowly moved closer in full strut.

I waited a while and tried some soft gobbler yelps. Again the bird gobbled, as did another tom that sounded to be about 150 yards behind me. The tom on the glade slowed, yet kept gobbling while the bird behind me rapidly closed the distance.

Meanwhile there I sat, in a small cluster of stones and bushes that didn't seem big enough to hide a bird dog, let alone a full-grown man.

By now the early morning sun had spread across the glade, causing the tom in front of me to glow as he strutted forty yards away. From the gobbles and drumming it sounded as if the gobbler behind me was only half as far off. I knew I couldn't move.

Even after the tom I was watching had closed into gun range I couldn't fire for fear of hitting one of the dozen or more hens surrounding him. So I waited, fully expecting to hear the loud alarm putts of the turkey behind me when he finally made out my shape. There was also another hen coming in from my left that could be a problem.

Finally one of the hens stopped and squatted; the old gobbler mounted her. The rest of the hens spread out a little, putting softly and running about the area. The whole thing seemed almost magical in the early morning light, the birds glistening and their shadows stretching across the glade.

The bred hen finally scurried from beneath the gobbler, causing him to stand and shake his feathers back into position. I putted and he stretched his head up one last time. The bird had spurs that were $1 \frac{5}{8}$ inches long.

I was still kneeling over the bird when the sound of a shot rolled in from Butch's direction. I sat on the glade for close to an hour, just enjoying the morning and the quality of the bird, and thinking of the good times the strutting area would hold in the future.

Unfortunately that strutting area is gone now, thanks to intensive lumbering and mining. But there are other strutting areas, and they will offer other memories yet to be made.

13
Gobblers With Hens

It's a sad, sad tale that's told around the campfires and backcountry cafés all across America's turkey country: "The gobblers aren't responding to calls. . . . They're still with the hens."

It is a common problem. Since spring seasons are set months or years in advance, a late spring will often find the tom courting the ladies that come running to him instead of going out to look for another party.

There are several signs that gobblers are with hens. Some are obvious: seeing them together in open fields or hearing the hens yelping and cutting around the gobbler on the roost.

Other possible indications are toms that gobble well on the roost, but then go silent when they've gathered their hens soon after flying down. Sometimes birds that respond but won't come in may already be with hens. Many hunters blame their calling, but you can't expect a gobbler to leave a sure thing for a blind date in the bush, even if she does sound as if she has a great personality.

Whenever I find myself competing with the real thing I usually forget all about the tom and start working on his hens. Bring them in and you can almost always count on the gobbler following them step for step.

The first thing you must realize is that talking with a hen is quite different from talking to a gobbler. You're sending completely different messages. While you're promising love to the gobbler, you're trying to tell the hen that you're the new girl on the block and you've come to take her date.

The key is to get her responding, then imitate what she does, only more aggressively with each conversation. If she yelps six times, you yelp eight times with just a little more feeling. If she starts cutting, you're in business.

Several years ago a client and I were well back into the Ozarks on a late-spring morning that had the gobblers surrounded by harems of willing hens. We'd failed to find a bird to work on the roost and our moving and calling hadn't gone well either.

Then about ten in the morning I got a single gobble. A little later a hen answered from the same direction. From then on the tom never made another sound, and the hen uttered only an occasional yelp. Realizing the problem for what it was, I simply sat back and went after the hen.

It took some aggressiveness, but I eventually got the hen cutting. Soon three or four other hens joined in. A couple of gobblers in different locations even entered into the shouting match.

The dominant hen finally made her move, running up the hill to our right, cutting and putting with every step. The rest of the hens—seven in all—were close behind.

My hunter did an excellent job of holding still and watching as the hens ran right past where we sat. A few seconds later came the big gobbler, strutting a few short steps, then hurrying to catch up. He never caught up.

I use this anecdote because it shows that it is possible to call hens, or even a group of them. Not a season passes that I don't bring in a tom simply by challenging his hens. There's no doubt in my mind that more good callers could do the same if they'd just develop the skills, then use them at the right time.

Sure, sometimes you call in hens that don't have a gobbler, but it's worth trying. Hold your ground, don't be afraid to call aggressively, and be alert. Remember that a few hunters out there are foolish enough to call as they sneak up on hen calls, so be alert and make positive identification.

I've taken a lot of gobblers that were with hens by relying on one of the gobbler's most predictable traits—a greed for sex. It's often possible to move in close to a bird that's roosted with hens and call him in as soon as he flies down.

As mentioned earlier, sneak in quietly well before fly-down time and give a few soft tree calls. When it starts getting lighter, increase the intensity of your calls. If you're set up where he's wanting to gather his

The adult hen turkey is also in the pecking order. Sometimes when a gobbler is with hens, you can get the hen to talk to you—when she comes in, the gobbler will follow. *Photo by Ray Eye.*

hens anyway, there's a strong chance that the gobbler might just fly down to get things started early.

If you can ever figure out a way to separate the gobbler from his hens, the odds will rapidly swing to your favor. If the gobbler's been having the time of his life for days and suddenly finds himself a bachelor he usually won't waste any time trying to get romancing again.

It's often possible to sneak up on a roosted flock and scare them by running at them, clapping, barking like a dog, or making some other noise. The key is to get close enough to force a good scatter. If the gobbler flies off with his hens you're no better off than before. But make him spend the night alone on a limb and he'll probably go berserk. The same scattering method works at sunrise as well.

If you've scattered the birds the night before, go ahead and work the

The gobbler following a hen to the hunter's position. *Photo by Ray Eye.*

bird on the limb the next morning. If you make a dawn scatter, let the woods settle for a few minutes, then call from a position between the gobbler and the hens—maybe even right at the roost. Be prepared for a bird that may literally run into your lap.

In the right situation you can fool a bird that's been snubbing your hen calls by hitting him with some gobbler talk. There was a time in my life when I killed a lot of dominant gobblers by gobbling at them with my voice. Let me tell you, it's a real experience to call a bird up when you know he's looking to hurt you!

But those days are gone. For one thing, there are really only a few short times of the year when a gobble will work, and it sometimes does more to scare sub-dominant toms than bring them in.

But the main reason it's not wise to use a gobble is because of safety. If you walk into an area full of hunters and you're the only creature gobbling, your life expectancy isn't too high. Then again, neither is your IQ.

But there is an alternative to gobbling at a bird: gobbler yelping. Until the past few years most people hadn't heard much about gobbler yelps, but I can remember toms that refused to budge at a hen call racing out to whip a yelping jake.

If you pay attention in the woods you'll hear both jakes and mature toms yelp, cut, purr, and make many of the same calls as hens. The difference is how they sound. There are exceptions, but most gobblers and jakes have a slower rhythm; their calls have fewer notes and are more drawn out than hen talk. Gobbler talk also seems to be a little deeper in pitch and much raspier than most hens.

For some reason a lot of hunters look on these gobbler calls as secondary tools, something nice to know but seldom used. In a way it's just the opposite. When the conditions are right—during the mating season—hen talk can be dynamite but at other times, it can be a bust.

But gobblers talk tom to tom twelve months out of the year. I've been calling gobblers in with gobbler talk during all four seasons for the past twenty years.

Gobbler yelps work for the same reason calling hen to hen works. The toms have a set pecking order, and if you try to squeeze into it some birds are going to get upset. Try using jake yelps when the mature birds are gobbling at each other and setting their pecking order. You'll see what I mean.

Believe me, there are times when a hen yelp just won't work, but gobbler yelping and cutting will bring the woods to life. A few seasons back a friend and I found ourselves working a tom that wouldn't leave his hens to cross a clearing to where we sat.

I had started off slow and easy, eventually building to some of my most aggressive hen cutting—but still no response. A few minutes later I let loose some gobbler yelps and cutting, and another bird opened up with the same thing back behind us. I wasted no time coming back a little longer and louder. With all of the gobbler talk the bird across the clearing started going crazy.

Both toms ended up running at us full speed. The one left his hens and was gobbling almost every step and the other yelped as many as twenty times in a row with some strings of seven or eight cuts mixed in. My hunter friend ended up taking the gobbling bird as he charged right at us.

As you can see, there are several ways to get around the gobbler-with-hens problem. The main idea is to accept the challenge and try something other than mating yelps.

And don't make the mistake of giving up too early. All turkeys go through the breeding cycle differently. While one tom may have a dozen hens, there may be a sub-dominant one just over the next ridge that doesn't have any.

Additionally, it's not at all uncommon for a tom to breed all of his hens early in the morning, then go looking for more later in the morning while the hens are on the nest.

If you work a bird at daybreak but can't get him into gun range, go back three or four hours later and give him a whirl. I've had a lot of these birds run right in to my first set of calls the second time around.

14
Late Spring

As mentioned earlier, a late spring is one of the most common problems turkey hunters face. Neither the turkeys nor the state game department is to blame; so all you can do is your best.

I've already mentioned such things as blind calling, using gobbler yelps, and handling toms that are with hens. One problem that can't be ignored is the lack of cover. I've seen a lot of spring seasons with no more underbrush than there was in December.

The lack of cover means you're going to be exposed for a much greater distance. In 1988 I heard a lot of complaints from hunters who said that a bird would gobble but would then shut up when they moved into a calling position. Personally, I think a lot of hunters were being seen.

When the woods are still open, it's important to keep your distance from a bird you're working. We had to set up close to a quarter of a mile away from the first gobbler that I called in for my brother Marty. The woods were so barren that we watched the bird come the last two hundred yards. I'm still amazed that an excited eleven-year-old held so still for so long.

If possible, keep some obstruction like the break of a ridge between you and the bird. It's also good to set up behind trees rather than in front of them.

You also have to adapt your calling. Locating calls aren't going to work well, and most of the calling that the turkeys do will be from gobbler to gobbler.

Keep your ears open for things other than gobbles and yelps. The sounds of two gobblers flapping and fighting carries for a long distance on still mornings. What that sound tells me is that there are at least two gobblers within hearing distance, their emotions are running high, and they're paying attention to something other than me.

I like to try to move in close to fighting gobblers. Once I hear the fight I'm up and moving in a hurry, since they can't hear or see well during the commotion. It surprises most hunters just how close you can get to fighting gobblers. I sure don't advise it, but I've gotten close enough to spook a nearby hen while the toms never missed a lick. The key is to waste no time, get close, and get ready.

I'll never forget one morning when a hunter and I walked our tails into the ground before we heard two birds gobbling at each other from adjoining ridges. I did my best to stir things up with aggressive calls. We hurried up an old logging road in hopes of intercepting the birds that were gobbling nonstop, but we got there too late.

One of the gobblers had crossed over to the other ridge and the fight was on. We could hear them thumping and flapping; so we wasted no time slipping over the saddle of the ridge where the birds couldn't see us and sneaked to within forty-five yards of the melee.

After a few minutes the toms rushed over the ridge and one flushed and sailed away. The other tom, the winner, went into a quick strut and sounded a triumphant gobble. I gave a few aggressive calls and he came right into range.

If the spring is really late you may find yourself facing winter flocks of gobblers. In such a situation, use fall calls and tactics. You can easily lure such flocks with gobbler yelps and cuts or you can split the flock and go after both halves.

The second year Mike Pearce and I hunted together the Missouri woods were barren and the gobblers still flocked up. About eight that morning I got onto a flock of eight or ten gobblers, eventually pulled them into range and shot a longbeard, thus scattering the rest of the flock.

An hour or so later Mike circled back into the area to find me and take some pictures. Stopping at the edge of a large glade, he gave a few long and drawn-out yelps. A gobbler responded. Before it was all over he had five toms closing in from three different directions. The one he tagged tipped the scales at twenty-two pounds.

Taking a spring gobbler is a challenge any time, let alone when mother nature throws you a curve. But remember that the longer and harder you hunt the higher your chances for success.

15
Birds In Bad Weather

Wind

Without a doubt a turkey hunter's biggest enemy is the wind. Ours is a sport that relies mostly on hearing and on being heard, both of which become harder in any wind at all. But you can still call turkeys in the wind if you're patient and thorough.

Here again, it's important to scout so that you can go where you know there are turkeys. Try to find a place that's out of the wind, like valleys and the windless side of hills.

Take your time and work the area well. Don't travel far between set-ups, and keep the wind at your back. Blind call for longer than you would on a calm day. Don't forget your box call, and make your calls loud. Strain your ears into the wind but don't get discouraged if you don't hear a gobble.

Turkeys can hear far better than we can, especially with the wind at our backs. On a day when the wind was twisting the Oklahoma cottonwoods to their roots, I watched a gobbler respond to every one of my calls from a hundred yards away. I never heard a note.

Be careful of your reaction when you finally do hear a bird respond to your calls. Because a heavy wind can distort calls, you can never be certain of a tom's exact location until you see him. It also works the other way around: the gobbler may have a little more trouble pinpointing your calls. Be patient and don't give up until the second you head for home. I've never seen the wind strong enough to blow the turkeys away.

Rain

The rain had come sometime during the night and seemed as though it intended to stay. It was coming down in a steady pour when I pulled my hat down tight and headed down the ridge. A gobbler answered my first hoots.

The turkey acted as if it was a beautiful, seventy-degree morning, gobbling at my hoots and soft yelps after I'd set up. He hit the ground with a gobble and headed toward me. The shot was less than twenty yards. I took my time leaving the woods, despite the continuing rain.

To be honest, I can't help but smile when I remember rainy-day turkey hunts. Like turkeys, no two such hunts have been alike except that there have been darned few that haven't produced their share of excitement.

But maybe one of the key reasons I like hunting in the rain is that it drives most hunters—some would say the most sensible hunters—from the woods. There's something special in knowing you're the only one around as you silently move over a dampened carpet of leaves.

It can also be a prime time to call and kill turkeys. Birds can't retreat to pickups or coffee shops. Rain is as much a part of their lives as sunshine and wind. Except in weather just short of a hurricane, they continue to move and feed in the rain. They'll also gobble and come to calls.

There are dozens of anecdotes I could choose from, but when I think of hunting in the rain my mind always fixes on a hunt I had with Pat Leonard. It wasn't just raining. It was flat out pouring all morning. We couldn't have been any wetter as we sloshed our way around the hardwood hills.

But our main problem was trying to hear—and be heard—in the rain. It pounded down so hard that it deadened any calls, both the birds' and ours. Still, we continued to move and call. Yanking a box call out of a bread wrapper, we huddled over it long enough to cut loose a long and loud series of calls before shoving it back into my pocket.

It got to where we weren't expecting to hear anything. When what sounded like a gobble cut through the roar of pouring water we both looked at each other, neither one of us wanting to say anything until we were sure the other had heard the same thing.

I took the call back out, hit a few more licks, and this time there was

Birds in Bad Weather

no mistaking the gobble. We sat there, our backs against trees while rain ran like waterfalls over the bills of our hats. We waited. Before long not one, but two gobblers came in, gobbling and strutting as if it were a still and sunny morning. Rounding a tree, the birds raised their heads, then fell as two shots sounded as one.

Whether or not you want to sit in the rain is up to you, but I don't think anyone should miss the half-hour before a storm system moves in. I can remember sitting on the mountain above my grandfather's place, watching a front approach from dozens of miles away. So many times woods that had sat silent since daybreak would come alive with the first distant rumblings of thunder. The closer the storm got, the more intense became the gobbling.

There were many times that we'd pile off the mountaintop, set up on a bird, take him, and still be back at the homestead for the first taps of rain on the old tin roof.

Even if you choose to sit out a shower, it's often best to stay in the area. Take a nap in your truck, play a quick game of cards, but don't miss what might become a good chance to work a gobbler.

For some reasons gobblers get as excited at the end of a rainstorm (or even just a lull between two storms) as they do at a system's approach. Find yourself in the woods at such a time and your chances for hearing gobblers are as good as at daybreak.

Early one morning I drove my old '64 GMC truck into the timber on a stormy morning that had put most creeks and gullies over their banks. Even the old two-track logging road that I followed from the main road was running like twin rivers in the beams of my headlights.

Between the wind and the rain, visibility couldn't have been more than a couple of hundred feet at daybreak. That, plus bolt after bolt of lightning, caused me to think twice about hunting. Within minutes I was asleep in the cab of my truck.

When I awakened the wind had all but died and the rain had softened to a gentle shower. Rolling down the window of the truck I could hear the sounds of turkeys gobbling throughout the valley below the ridge.

I simply picked the closest bird, moved to a good calling position, fired him up, and took him when he came up. The torrents of rain hit again just as I made it back to the truck.

The key to hunting in the rain is to rely on your common sense. If you have decent rain equipment and there's no lightning, then you may want to go ahead and hunt. Don't get discouraged if the birds aren't gobbling. A lot of bad weather toms come in silently.

But they still come to calls. After all, they only get to play this mating

If the weather is affecting the gobbler's reaction to your hen calling, try changing the situation by fall-calling the spring gobbler. Instead of calling hen to gobbler, you use gobbler yelps to call gobbler to gobbler. *Photo by Ray Eye.*

game for a few weeks of the year and they're not likely to let a little water get in their way. As I see it, neither will most good turkey hunters.

Snow

    A slow, steady rain made for a slippery climb as John Hauer and I left his Suburban and hiked up into the Black Hills. By the time we reached the top of the ridge the raindrops were bigger, splatting down in the form of slush.

    We continued along the ridge, stopping every so often to send a series of calls down the slopes. By the time we reached our third or fourth calling position it was beginning to snow. The longer we hunted the harder it fell.

    Two hours after dawn a bird gobbled and I started calling from behind a huge ponderosa. Two toms, a jake, and a mature bird came over the lip of the ridge, the bigger bird strutting for all he was worth.

    But then it hit me. Because of the treacherous walking I hadn't moved a shell from my magazine to the chamber of my shotgun. By some minor miracle I managed to accomplish that task, but when I went to take aim the jake spooked and the big gobbler ducked out of sight.

By then it was snowing hard, with flakes the size of quarters dropping from the sky. After a good laugh at my forgetfulness, Hauer and I moved to the next ridge and set up. This time there was no gobble, just three red and blue heads coming over the ridge after my first series of calls.

We were now sitting in what was becoming a full-fledged blizzard. I took the first tom to offer a clear shot and we headed off the hill, leaving tracks in the snow behind us.

As you can see, turkey hunting in snow has never really posed many problems for me, or even for other hunters like Hauer who have to deal with it every year. For most hunters it's little more than a temporary freak of nature, a phenomenon that will pass in a few hours.

I don't think turkeys notice any difference between snow and rain. Several Missouri openers have seen up to three inches of snow, yet thousands of hunters still take birds.

Depending on the conditions, sometimes the toms gobble as if all is normal. Other times they play the game quietly, still coming to calls but doing so either without gobbling or with just a few gobbler yelps.

Snow is like any other weather-related problem, in that you have to realize the limitations and keep hunting. If the birds aren't gobbling well, then set up and blind call in some of your favored locations. If they don't respond to spring mating calls, try some fall calls like gobbler yelps, or soft talk like quiet purrs and clucks.

Keep trying and sooner or later you'll succeed, something you can't do from the warm confines of a camper or coffee shop.

16
Hunting Pressure

The growing popularity of spring turkey hunting is one of the old good news-bad news situations. On the positive side it's good that more people are having fun, and the increase in hunters provides more help in challenging anything that would hurt our sport. It also creates more money for state game departments and such organizations as the National Wild Turkey Federation.

It also means there's going to be a lot more competition in the woods—especially on public ground—and that can cause a ton of problems. One way to avoid them is to gain access to private property where not much hunting is allowed. It takes some work, and in a few areas a little money, but the access can be worth the time and cash.

It's best to start checking into private ground well before the season. I'm talking months, not days or even weeks—the sooner the better. Try to focus on areas well away from major roads and as far from major cities as possible. Also avoid areas that are known for their great turkey hunting. Your chances of gaining access and having a quality hunt are often far greater in areas with only a mediocre turkey population.

But no matter where you hunt, there's always a chance that you'll run into some competition; so it pays to be prepared. The key is to go one step further than the other hunters.

Knowing the woods and the turkeys within them can be more critical than ever on heavily hunted grounds. Try to be there waiting when that gobbler pitches off the roost. Also, identify the areas with the most hunting pressure. Look for little, out-of-the-way pockets of timber and make the extra effort to stay away from other hunters—for their sake as well as yours.

It's also wise to change the hunt pattern. If most hunters are parking on one stretch of road and walking in from the east, then find a way to come in from the west.

Sometimes it's possible to float a canoe into desolate backcountry that's free of hunters. Other times you have to take a boat across a lake to get the surrounding woods all to yourself. Some national forests also allow you to backpack to areas too remote for most hunters.

Remember, the main goal is to be unique, to keep from blending into the crowd of hunters the turkeys are so used to. I avoid hunting weekends and opening days on public ground. I've also returned to places on a weekday late in the season and have had an entire national forest pretty much to myself.

The same thing goes for time of day as well. The woods may be packed at sunrise but nearly free of hunters by ten or eleven that morn-

A canoe is an excellent way to reach birds far back in the woods. Where legal, it is also good for floating rivers, stopping often to listen and call for gobblers. *Photo by Mike Pearce.*

ing. Also, if you think most hunters are hen yelping on diaphragm calls, then try cutting and purring on a box or a slate call, and don't forget the gobbler yelps.

Several years ago David Crowe of Alabama and I headed into some heavily hunted woods about an hour before the noon quitting time. Preseason scouting had shown a dominant bird set up on a long ridge. Unfortunately the road beside the ridge looked like a parking lot most early mornings.

David and I quietly worked our way to the heart of the bird's territory, sat down, and took a short nap to make sure things had settled down. Using a slate call, I let loose some purrs and real soft yelps. After several long minutes the bird gobbled.

A little later I tried some more hen calls. The bird gobbled but I could tell he was more than a little paranoid. Forgetting the hen calls, I waited a few minutes, then used my voice to hit the tom with some real aggressive gobbler yelps. The bird's approach wasn't overly exciting, but the fact that he weighed 23½ pounds, had an 11½-inch beard and 1½-inch spurs more than made up for it.

Working birds that have been spooked several times for days on end often means using a lot more patience and a slightly different style of calling. I usually move shorter distances and stay longer. It also helps to keep the calls a little softer, imitating a hen that's just as nervous as the gobbler. Sometimes I scratch the leaves with my hands to further convince an old gobbler that I'm a real hen and not another hunter. If the tom's real close, I may forget about calling and simply scratch the leaves.

Where there's lots of pressure from hunters, you can expect less gobbling and toms that often simply show up when you're blind calling. Keep in mind that gobbling brings competition; don't encourage it. I seldom use locating calls on crowded hunting areas.

Also, it's important that you know how to deal with other hunters in the area. If a hunter comes in and spooks a bird that you're working, screaming at the guy isn't going to help (even if it does make you feel a heck of a lot better).

I've taken several spooked birds by waiting fifteen to thirty minutes, then calling softly like a nervous hen that was spooked but is still interested.

A friend, Jack Hessler, and I once found four vehicles parked near a good bird's territory in a small patch of timber between a river and a major county road. Knowing that the bird was probably already spooked we headed to town for breakfast.

At half past ten we cruised the area and noted that the cars were gone. We parked well down the road and quietly circled back to the place

Turkey gobblers will sometimes hide by squatting down in weeds or grass when they hear an approaching hunter. In Alabama, I saw strutting gobblers lie down in the grass until a truck passed and then raise back up into strut. *Photo by Ray Eye.*

I'd heard the gobbler before the season. Again, I opted for a slate call and some very light clucks and purrs followed by some nervous yelps. The bird only gobbled once but he walked right up to Jack, who took him.

It's important to keep in mind that there are other hunters in the woods. There are times when you may want to go to some lengths to keep other hunters from working or spooking your bird. One night two of us intentionally spooked an old double-beard from his roost near two well-traveled roads.

At daylight several trucks stopped, hooted or crow called, then left when they got no response. We, on the other hand, set up right at the original roost tree and used hen calls to bring the bird into gun range.

But you need to keep things in perspective when you're in the woods with a lot of other hunters. If the ground is public, or even if it's private and other hunters have permission, they have just as much right to be there as you do.

If you can hear others working a bird, sit tight and see what happens. Don't spook the bird someone's working just so he can't have a chance at it. There are more than enough turkeys to go around.

And as always, be careful and think of safety at all times.

17

Hangups

Events don't always progress as planned in the turkey woods. The hunts we dream about—birds gobbling at anything and running right to calls—are usually in the minority.

But success can still be yours. With a little understanding, a little more work, and a little luck, you can manage to outsmart an old gobbler no matter what he throws at you.

One of the most exciting, yet most frustrating, experiences you can have is working a bird that gobbles, maybe even double-gobbles, at every one of your calls, but won't come in. Sometimes he'll cover part of the distance, sometimes he won't budge an inch, and sometimes he'll even head directly away from you, still gobbling at every sound.

After talking with hundreds of frustrated hunters, I've decided that poor calling position is to blame for the majority of hangups. Many of them can be attributed to fences, deep ditches, creeks, highways, thick brush, or anything else that a gobbler simply doesn't want to cross.

The easiest cure for such hangups is to eliminate them before they happen. Get as close as the terrain will allow and make it as easy as possible for the turkey to get to you.

But there are also times when a gobbler simply wants to hold his ground, probably thinking it would be easier for the hen to come to him. Often simply changing calls or callers makes the difference on such a bird.

The bird that's standing just out of gun range may come on in if he hears the soothing talk of purrs and clucks. Just the reverse may work on the gobbler that's stuck to one spot farther away: hit him with some hot cutting and he might just become unglued and come on in.

There have been times when I've turned my head and called, imitating a hen that is walking away. The gobbler often goes berserk and comes sprinting in. There have also been times when I've gone mute for fifteen to twenty minutes to bring an uncooperative bird right on in. I've also used a jake yelp or two to get a dominant gobbler so mad that he has to come in to get things straightened out.

The main idea is to feel free to try something a little different if you're sure what you've been doing isn't working.

No matter why a bird won't come in—if there's a barrier in his way or he's just being bullheaded—you may see him come right on in if you simply change locations.

It's tough to tell when to move on a gobbling bird. I've moved at the wrong time, only to see the bird gobbling from my former location within a minute after my departure.

But if the bird is definitely heading the other way or hasn't moved any closer for quite some time, then it might be time to ease into a new location.

Back away from where you were calling and go around the bird. If the bird is leaving and going in a set direction then I quietly hustle around until I'm ahead of him, then try him again. Get between him and his destination and the odds are in your favor.

Sometimes all you have to do is set up on another side of the bird—especially if he would rather not cross some obstacle—and he'll work just fine.

Then again, hunt long enough and you'll run across a gobbler that's totally uncooperative; he won't come because he simply doesn't want to. All you can do is either go to another bird or keep trying with the same one. Sometimes persistence pays off.

It's been about a dozen years since I worked a bird on a morning cold enough for my jeep to break ice on the mud puddles as I followed a curving route toward the top of an Ozark mountain.

I eased the jeep to a stop not far from where a saddle and a series of glades joined this mountain with another. Through the years it had been a place to hear a number of gobblers, but on that frosty morning there was but a single tom gobbling. But oh, was he ever gobbling.

I started him on the limb with a hoot and he gobbled at it. He

This adult eastern gobbler has chosen the edge of a cattle pasture and will not come to the calls of the hunter. A lot of hangups can be avoided by learning the lay of the land and the habits of the gobblers you are hunting. *Photo by Ray Eye.*

gobbled at every one of my hen calls when he hit the ground, but then wouldn't budge. It didn't make any difference whether I used my voice, slate, diaphragm, or box call; the bird wouldn't come in. Then again he wouldn't shut up either.

We traded calls for quite a while before the gobbler slowly started moving away. "No problem," I thought, "I'll circle him and then it'll be all over." Wrong. I made my circle, hit him with a box call and he gobbled but wouldn't move. Soon he was gobbling at every purr, cut, or yelp. Then he started moving in a different direction again.

I moved four more times on this bird and always had the same reaction. I tried calling nearly nonstop and I tried total silence but he wouldn't even begin to come in. No matter where I was he slowly started moving steadily away.

I decided to try one more time. Moving in at about the same level, I made a soft voice tree call. The bird turned and sprinted right to me.

As far as I know, the twenty-two-pound tom with inch-plus spurs hadn't seen hunters that season, and he didn't have any hens with him either. I also know that I never spooked him. So it goes with turkeys. All you can do is keep trying.

18
Blind Calling

Just because you don't hear a gobble doesn't mean a bird won't respond to your calls. A lot of sub-dominant gobblers that have gotten their stuffing knocked out every time they sound off may come running to a call without ever making a sound. The same goes for birds that are under a lot of pressure or aren't at the peak of the breeding season.

No matter what the reason, if the birds simply aren't gobbling, your best bet is to move and blind call. I hate to sound like a broken record, but if possible stick to the high country where you can be heard, and go where your scouting has proven there are gobblers.

Knowing how long to sit in one place, though, is the big question and it's one that I can't definitely answer. I've sat in one place for an hour without seeing or hearing anything, then flushed a bird that was coming in the second I stood up.

If you have a lot of confidence in an area and the birds simply aren't gobbling, it doesn't hurt to blind call for thirty to forty-five minutes. If one spot doesn't pan out, then keep moving until you've covered your entire hunting area. The important thing is to keep a positive attitude and your senses on full alert at all times.

Listen for sounds like turkeys walking and gobblers spitting and drumming. Pay attention to the wildlife around you. The scoldings of

This adult gobbler came in silently, late in the morning. The hunter called him into gun range by moving from position to position throughout his hunting area. *Photo by Ray Eye.*

squirrels, crows, and blue jays may reveal the location of an approaching gobbler.

Keep your eyes open for any sign of turkeys moving in your direction, no matter how bored or miserable you are. Several years ago one of the few days I didn't have a client dawned cloudy and cold with a slushy snow that soaked everything. The first place I hunted was totally silent except for the sounds of dripping water and the occasional chatter of my teeth as I tried spot after spot.

By midmorning I was trying to thaw out in my jeep as I headed toward the country I know better than any other — the public ground I had roamed as a boy near my grandfather's farm.

Things didn't look too promising as I slipped and slided my way around the hills. The area had been hunted hard and the birds weren't gobbling well when it was warm and sunny, let alone freezing cold and overcast.

My first two set-ups were total busts, which only got me soaked and shivering again. Calling position number three was a series of small, overgrown fields that sat nestled between a jagged series of ridges.

I'd been there what seemed like ten hours, probably closer to ten minutes, and was just about to pack it in for good when something out of the ordinary caught my ear. I sat silently and strained my ears. There it was again—the low, vibrating noise of a drumming gobbler. I slipped out a few more soft notes and then shut up.

Staring out into the gloom I could barely make out the tops of five adult turkey fans coming over a slight rise in front of me. Except for the drumming, the gobblers moved as silently as ghosts as they closed the distance. The longbeard I took from the bunch was far from my biggest, but he's darned sure one of my most memorable.

19
The Buddy System

In most cases turkey hunting is best as a solitary sport. Your chances for success are far better when you can move quietly and without delay, making all of your own decisions. For some reason two people seem to make as much noise as three or four. And you also have to worry about what the other hunter is doing or thinking.

But then again there are times when it's best to buddy-up for turkey hunting. Over the years I've called up far more turkeys for friends and clients than for myself.

Often it's best to double-up when a hunter is new to the sport. Turkey hunting can be frustrating enough for veterans, let alone rank amateurs. I encourage all good hunters to share a little of what they've learned with beginners. If an experienced hunter has a close friend or relative who's new to the sport, he may want to take him along on a hunt or two.

Most of the time this boils down to having one hunter and one shooter. In other words, the more experienced of the two will be doing everything from picking the calling sights to actually calling the bird.

How you handle such a situation depends largely on the experience of the new hunter. If he's totally in the dark about the sport, the caller will want to leave his own gun at home and concentrate solely on helping the beginner.

Turkey hunting is usually best done solo, but there are times when the buddy system works well. Here Ray is calling for a friend. *Photo by Mike Pearce.*

In such situations I like the hunter sitting right in my lap with his back against my chest so that I can whisper directions and instructions right into his ear.

If the hunter has some experience—that is, if he can tell a gobbler from a hen, knows what to listen for, and is undoubtedly safe—I usually put him at a tree up in front of me. Sometimes I may set the hunter up quite far ahead of my calling position.

You see, a turkey's hearing is so accurate that he can all but pinpoint exactly where the hen calls are coming from. If he thinks he's moving toward a hen that's fifty yards away he won't be paying as close attention to the trees that are right beside him. That takes much of the pressure off the gunner when he goes to make his move. For bowhunters, it's an unbelievable advantage.

Having the caller some distance behind the gun is also a good way to fool shy turkeys that have been hanging up out of range. In every turkey hunter's career there are birds that will charge right up to fifty yards, where they'll stand their ground and gobble until their heads hurt. While the guy with the call may be out of luck, his buddy—thirty yards out in front — is in fine shape. Locating the gunner between the gobbler and the caller also gives the caller more freedom to use friction calls or to use his hands to throw calls to one side or another.

Sometimes it even pays for the caller to be up and moving when working a gobbler. If you're calling to a gobbler that's not showing a lot of interest, sometimes you can get his attention by backing away, but continuing to call. Sometimes such a bird will simply forget about you, but many times he'll have his ego crushed just enough to give chase.

Another little trick is for the caller to pull a wary, circling gobbler right past the hunter. For instance, if the gobbler is coming in from the left, I move toward the right. If he angles too far to the right, then I slip back to the left.

Running interference with other hunters is another job for a good partner. It may be as simple as standing on a country road and warning hunters wandering by or it may mean actually stopping someone who's trying to move in and set up on the gobbling bird.

Scott Minner couldn't have been much more than eleven years old when I took him on a Missouri hunt a few years ago. We'd been planning the hunt for almost a year, and all that time the hunt was on Scott's mind. My plan was to make it one he'd never forget.

Things couldn't have begun any better in our dreams. We heard a lot of gobbling at daybreak and I was able to pull two good gobblers into range, . . . but Scott missed.

Later that morning we met up with John Bostick and were lucky enough to fire up another gobbler in another area. At first Scott didn't even want to move in on the bird with us. He kept saying that he'd had his chance and blown it, and that now was the time for me to call one up for John.

We finally talked him into coming and moved to a saddle where two ridges met. I set John up on the ridge with the gobbling turkey and sat Scott a little farther down the other ridge. As luck would have it, a bird opened up on that ridge as well.

I backtracked to the logging road that crossed the saddle, then called toward one bird and then the other. The birds were gobbling well and coming. My main concern was that someone would come in and mess things up.

Sure enough, the sounds of another caller started coming closer and closer down the old road. When the hunter walked within sight I recognized him and explained the situation. He politely sat down to listen to the action.

I kept calling but the birds grew quiet. Then there was a shot from Scott's direction. John was already standing beside Scott and a good gobbler by the time I got to him. As long as I live I'll never forget what the kid said as I walked up. "I, I, I really didn't want to shoot him. Mr. Eye. I wanted John to have a chance," he said sheepishly. Then breaking into a smile he added, "but when that gobbler walked right up to twenty yards he was history!"

It's also good to have an extra hunter when you're blind calling and the birds are coming in quietly. As long as both hunters keep still, two sets of eyes can watch a lot more ground than one.

One of the neatest, though rarely used, tricks of the buddy system is working a gobbler that is obviously call-shy. Well, maybe call-petrified would be a better term for the gobbler I'm thinking of.

There was one old gobbler I'd worked for several mornings that would come off a ridge gobbling but never get any closer. He'd cover a lot of ground from left to right, then back again, but he simply refused to come any closer to my calls. If I got up and moved a little closer, the turkey would head in the exact opposite direction.

I played his little game for a couple of mornings before I decided it was time to play dirty. Ron Lawson and I got to the ridge well before daylight. When I hooted the bird gobbled. I decided to have Ron hold his ground while I circled around the ridge to the opposite side of the turkey.

Just as he had done every other morning, the bird gobbled at everything, moving from side to side but not coming any closer. And just like every other morning, when I moved a little closer the bird headed the other way.

Then I decided it was time to get even. Knowing Ron's approximate location, I gradually moved my calling sites toward the bird, almost driving him like a herd of cattle. I'd move fifty yards closer, and his next gobble would come from fifty yards farther down the ridge. He played the game well, until he walked past the spot where Ron was waiting.

20

The Harvest

Every year hundreds of hunters do well in the game of getting a gobbler—up until the final seconds. They locate the bird and call him into range only to miss an opportunity. No matter how far you work a turkey, the last few yards into gun range are the most critical.

Even if you know the bird is close, it's important to keep both eyes open and your head up and off the gun stock until just before the shot for better visibility. Whatever you do, don't turn your head unless you absolutely have to.

Keep your ears on full alert. Listen for the sounds of turkeys walking in the leaves and the telltale spit and drum of a strutting gobbler.

Use your eyes to scan the area in front of you. Pick the area apart bit by bit. I've called dozens of turkeys to within shooting range and found my guest unable to see them because he was either looking for the whole bird, looking too close, or looking too far.

Look for pieces of the bird: the red, white and/or blue head of a gobbler peeking up over a log, or maybe a pair of feet on the other side of a big cedar. Don't expect the bird to be somewhere; expect him to be anywhere.

It's critical that you make absolute identification before you even think about shooting. You have to rule out every other possibility: a dog, a person, an illegal hen.

If the turkey is coming directly toward your position, be patient and let him come into good range for your gun's capabilities. Don't shoot too soon or at long distances. The excitement of the sport is in fooling the gobbler on his own ground and bringing him in very close for a clean kill. *Photo by Ray Eye.*

In the spring, make sure the bird's beard is visible, but don't panic once you see that it is a legal tom. If you can see him, he can see any move you make, and that means you shouldn't turn your head, move your gun, or shift your body.

Hold all movement until the bird's head is behind something like a tree or fanned tail. Regardless, make all moves slow and fluid. If you can, act only while the bird is moving, when it's the hardest for him to pinpoint anything.

The Harvest 143

Be sure the gobbler is well within your killing range and don't take any chancy shots. Be patient and your time will come.

The same goes for a bird that for some reason comes in behind you. Play the waiting game, and he'll probably come around. If he doesn't, go ahead and let him walk away. Once he's gone, adjust your position and then call him back.

I should add, though, that a good calling position will solve the problem of the bird coming in from behind. Additionally, the bird that you think is at your back may well be an entirely different bird.

Always be aware that another turkey may come in unseen and unheard. If such a bird spooks, keep your composure, because all is not lost. The putting of an alarmed bird may add more fire to the gobbler you're working. I've sometimes copied the alarm call of such a bird and the tom kept coming. Other times I've moved a small distance, sat silently for twenty to thirty minutes, and restarted the gobbler.

Never, never shoot a turkey when he is in strut and his head is all pulled back into his body: a shot at such a small area could mean a wounded turkey. Wait. He'll stick his head up to look for the hen. If he

Never shoot a gobbler when he is full strut. There is not much of a target with his head pulled back into his body. Many turkeys are crippled every year when shot in strut. The gobbler is looking for a hen—wait for him to raise his head. Or you can make a putting sound to get him to raise out of the strut. *Photo by Ray Eye.*

Get to a downed bird quickly, but don't do anything dangerous like run through the woods with a loaded gun. This hunter moves up quickly, ready for a second shot if needed. *Photo by Mike Pearce.*

doesn't, give a sharp putt. If you're not using a diaphragm call just do the best you can with your lips. Either way, he'll raise his head like a periscope to see what's going on, exposing all of his head and neck.

If you have a loud safety on your gun, use one finger on each side of the button to slowly slide it through quietly. If your gun has a hammer, hold the trigger until the hammer has eased back into its locked position.

Be sure that your head is down on the gun and your cheek is where it should be, and that you're aiming the shotgun as if it were a rifle. Aim for the turkey's cherry-sized wattles and squeeze the trigger.

If the gobbler's within gun range and your gun is shooting as it should the bird will be yours.

Despite what everyone else says, don't run to the bird. Running through the woods with a loaded gun can be pure suicide, even if the bird is only twenty yards away. Sure, you don't want to waste any time, but you need to be sure you have an open shot if the bird tries to get back up.

There's nothing wrong with an insurance shot, but be careful where you place it. I talked with one hunter who called a bird up and shot it, and it went down. When his partner ran up to within five yards of the gobbler, it started the usual flopping and the youngster unloaded his three-inch 12-gauge right into the bird's body. So much for a decent meal.

If the bird is still flopping, go ahead and put your foot on his neck until he stops. Sometimes the shock to his nervous system may keep him bouncing for a while. Look at the bird's eyes. If they're still open and blinking you may want to break his neck or even step back, aim a few inches in front of his beak, and give him another shot.

Never pick a bird up before he's totally lifeless. Darned near every turkey hunter I know has gotten excited and grabbed a big tom by his legs, only to be thrashed by the bird's spurs. Others have had less painful but equally interesting encounters.

John Hauer tells about guiding a pair of hunters on his Turkey Track Ranch in South Dakota's Black Hills. It was one of those mornings when everything seemed to be going right. John brought a jake up at first light and one of the hunters dropped it like a rock.

Wanting to get the other hunter a bird while they were still gobbling, Hauer rushed out to the jake, looked it over, and stuffed in his back pouch. A little later that morning Hauer was working another hot bird when all hell broke loose.

The flopping of the bird in his pouch almost knocked him over. When the jake broke free of the pouch, his head was up and his feet were moving. Hauer made a grab for the bird's neck, which started a wrestling match that the guide barely won, and not without a good flogging. Remember that he was still trying to call in the other gobbler the entire time! He finally did get the second bird into range only to have his hunter miss it clean. Some days are shineola and some days are. . . .

21

Fall Hunting

Over the years I have heard dozens, maybe hundreds, of turkey hunters make negative comments about the fall turkey season. Most claim that without the big birds gobbling it just isn't exciting enough. I disagree.

For a while one late-October morning nothing happened to dispel their resistance. Clinton Steele and I had split up to work opposite sides of a river that divided his northern Missouri property.

Total darkness turned to full light without a sound and with no sight of the four longbeards we'd seen the previous day. I started off with some soft gobbler yelps at first light. Now, close to an hour later, I'd built to an aggressive series of calls with fifteen to twenty yelps.

Sitting with my back against an old tree at the edge of a logging road, I was alternately sending calls to the left and to the right. My confidence with the spot had all but disappeared when I sent one more set of yelps to the left. That's when I first saw them, the four large birds trotting across a clearing a hundred yards away.

By the time I slid around to face them I could hear the gobblers cutting as they closed the distance. I let loose some aggressive cutting and gobbler yelping. One of the toms stood erect, flapped his wings and quickened his pace.

The toms were gradually skirting to my left when they came into gun range. The first of the flock trotted right past me and the next two were a little too far to the left. The back bird was at the fringe of gun range and coming right at me. I slowly pointed my gun and hoped he'd keep coming.

Out of the corner of my eye I could see two of the toms pacing back and forth. They called from time to time as they searched for the source of the calls they'd followed. The problem was the lead bird. He had looped in behind me and I could hear him walking closer and closer. By then I was done calling and was trying to hold as still as the tree that was supporting my awkward slouch.

The crunching in the leaves grew louder and louder until I was sure the gobbler could be no more than a few feet away. Finally sensing something was wrong, he took off running and putting. Hearing the commotion, the bird in front of me raised his head at twenty-eight steps. I pulled the trigger when the bead of my Remington settled on his neck. The 20½-pound tom folded at the shot.

I moved up quickly and admired the bird and his 10-inch beard. But it was quite a while before my nerves were calmed enough to head for the truck.

I remember wondering how anyone could not call such a hunt exciting and rank it right up with the best of spring memories.

Maybe the reason a lot of people don't get too fired up about fall hunting is because they simply don't understand it very well. Most states started their spring seasons years before their fall seasons, which meant hunters learned first of gobbling birds and hen calling.

Actually the fall hunt is turkey hunting for *real* turkeys. Their actions and behavior are typical for 300 days out of a year. Behavior in the mating season is the exception. Yet a hunter steps into the fall woods, makes a few seductive yelps, and wonders why he doesn't get a gobble, consequently concluding that fall is a second rate season. I think he's dead wrong.

The key to having fun in the fall is understanding the turkeys and what they're doing. This is often a time of flocks that range from two to two dozen or more turkeys. Understanding and knowing how to take advantage of the bird's gregarious nature is the first step to success.

During a year that has a good hatch, many of the flocks are made up of hens with poults. Sometimes there is only one hen and her brood, but there may be up to four or five mature hens with a mob of poults milling around.

Still caught between adolescence and adulthood, groups of jakes often band together and wander the woods. Again, they can number anywhere from a pair to a dozen or more shortbeards in one bunch.

Barren hens (those that didn't raise a brood) will often band together in a similar manner.

Then there are the old longbeards. Occasionally an old patriarch is off by himself, but more often a mature tom accompanies a bachelor flock of similar birds.

But always keep in mind that there are no absolutes in turkey hunting, especially in fall flocks. Almost any combination is possible. I've seen longbeards with hens and poults. You're liable to see a jake running with anything that will tolerate it. Late in the fall it's not uncommon to see turkeys of all ages and both sexes in one huge flock.

The important idea to remember is that each bird out there has its place in the pecking order. Even late-hatched poults no bigger than barnyard chickens have their dominant bird. Turkeys relate to pecking order every week of the year. The hunter who knows how to use that fact to his advantage can have a great hunt in the fall.

You see, in the spring you usually call from one sex to the other, but in the fall you often call from like bird to like bird, such as from poult to poult or old tom to old tom. (One exception is calling like a hen to regroup a scattered brood.) All, and I mean all, types of birds can be called in the fall if you simply speak their language. But first you have to find a bird to talk to.

Scouting is as important in the fall as it is in the spring. In fact, getting out and walking the woods is imperative because there usually will be no booming gobbles that can be heard for long distances.

With a fresh crop of leaves and mast on the ground, any scratchings should be easy to see. You should also keep an eye out for the usual droppings, tracks, and feathers. In traditional hardwood forests, check oak groves for evidence of feeding flocks. If there's a lot of agriculture and little mast, check places like corn and soybean fields. Fall turkeys will normally be found wherever the food is.

Be sure to keep your ears open whenever you're scouting in the woods. Listen for the sounds of calling hens or the wingbeats of a flock flying up or down from a roost.

In some parts of the country it's possible to do some scouting with binoculars, looking for birds that are feeding in the open. Since fall birds sometimes have very regular behavior patterns, talking with deer or squirrel hunters or local farmers can often put you in the right area.

As in the spring, some of your best prospects are birds on the roost. If you've done your homework you may already know the general location of a roosted flock.

If you're starting from scratch, get to high ground and listen carefully for turkey talk. Most people are surprised at the amount of yelping, purring, and other conversation at a fall roost. If you don't hear anything from your post, try a few kee-kee runs. There aren't many hens in the woods that can resist the pleading calls of a lost poult, especially when they're on the roost.

The basic approach for working a fall roost is the same as for the spring. Get as close to the birds as possible and try to be situated where the turkeys will want to land.

If you listen well, you should be able to tell which bird is doing the most calling. You should then call directly to that bird, remembering to call from like bird to like bird.

Do whatever that turkey is doing but with a little more intensity. If it yelps three times, you yelp five times. If it starts cutting, you cut right back. Chances are, the excitement will get the other birds calling too. When that happens you're in for a lot of fun.

Over the years, including back before Missouri had a fall season when I called just for fun and photos, I'll bet I've worked several hundred groups of birds on the roost, ranging from a single bird to a flock of close to forty. One particular hunt comes to mind.

A hen had cut my kee-kee whistles just down the ridge from where my client and I were waiting. Moving quickly, we set up slightly above the bird about seventy yards away.

As it began to get light, what sounded like the same hen started with some soft talk, and I joined the conversation. In the space of a few minutes we went from soft purrs and clucks to aggressive cutting. Soon it sounded as if the treetops in front of us were filled with excited turkeys.

When it got light enough to see well, I let out one more aggressive string of calls. The sound of beating wings literally filled our ears. The turkeys hit the ground calling excitedly and we could hear them moving about to regroup.

I gave the birds a few minutes to get together and quiet down while my client got his gun up on his knee and settled into a comfortable position.

The woods grew still when I let out some soft purrs. All hell broke loose when I followed with some aggressive yelps, then cutting. The flock literally charged up the hill, the dominant hen in the lead cutting nonstop while the other birds sounded intermittent excited calls.

Within seconds the whole mob was milling about in front of us. My client wisely took a young gobbler standing off to the side of the main bunch.

Flock Calling

Much of what's been written about calling fall turkeys advocates walking the soles off your boots until you find a flock, then scattering it

A fall hunter's dream: a group of young birds that have been separated from the hen. Such birds will often run to good calling. *Photo by Mike Pearce.*

to the four corners of the earth. To my mind, there's no sense in chasing off a bunch of turkeys you walked miles to find. And you could have called them to you in the first place.

Turkeys don't always need to be scattered to be called. They're pretty social, and they'll more than likely want to investigate any new kid on the block that they hear. Again, the hardest part is often finding the turkeys to call.

I like to move and call much as I do in the spring. I'll pick an area that scouting has shown to have a good population, then work the ridges, setting up every few hundred yards or as far away as my last calls may have carried.

The basics are the same: try to set up where your calls can be heard simultaneously in several good areas. Get comfortable and let the woods settle down before you start calling. Start off with soft and short calls in case there's a flock just over the ridge. As time progresses, make your calls more aggressive.

Remember that in the fall the sexy mating yelps might not do much good. If you're in a state that lets fall hunters take any bird and you aren't choosy, use a lot of kee-kee whistles until you get an old hen to answer. Then imitate her response.

Don't rely too much on a smooth sounding diaphragm call, especially if you're after mature birds. A good slate call that can produce deep purrs and aggressive putts and yelps can work well, as can a box call. If you're going to use a mouth call, stick with something that's got a raspy sound to it, like a call with a split reed. At least it works well for me.

As in the spring, you can expect each turkey to respond to calls in different ways. Some open up and come in screaming like kamikazes. Others take their time and come in without muttering a sound.

Really use your ears. Many hunters, conditioned to the booming gobbles of spring, have problems hearing some of the soft purrs and putts of a fall bird. Listen for the sounds of turkeys walking in the dry leaves.

Since they're coming for reasons other than sex, fall turkeys may or may not be a little slower to respond than spring birds. If you have some confidence in your location, and if you know there are turkeys in the area, be prepared to wait forty-five minutes to an hour. Always scan the area thoroughly before getting up quietly and slowly to move to your next calling station.

As with all turkey hunts, keep your eyes and ears open when trying to locate a fall flock. Sometimes you'll get a response but the birds won't come in. There could be a barrier between you and the birds that they don't want to cross, or perhaps the birds' daily routine takes them in the other direction. Either way, by changing calling locations, you may get them to come right in.

If the turkeys are in traditional hardwoods feeding on nuts you can often literally track them down. A few years ago a friend and I were working a big tract of national forest, but were coming up with a whole lot of nothing before we happened upon some fairly fresh turkey scratchings near an old logging road.

Figuring the direction of the flock, we worked our way down the logging road, stopping to set up where we could send calls to both sides of the road.

Our first few calling sights brought no answers to my calls, but we noticed that the scratchings were beginning to look much fresher. Our fourth set-up was at the junction of the logging road and another road. I made a soft call and a turkey answered from what sounded like fifty yards in front of us. I cut and yelped back at the bird and the entire flock of about twenty-five turned and came running. My partner took a young bird at about ten feet.

There are times, such as when you're in an area that you haven't scouted well, when trying to find a flock of turkeys to work is frustrating. Often all of the birds for a mile or more may congregate in one area of a certain field or grove of oaks.

All you can do is keep moving and calling until you either strike birds or run out of daylight. But don't give up. The turkeys have to be somewhere, and if they're all in one spot the hunt can really get exciting.

Mark Lowder and I once moved and called all day to hear but a few distant hen yelps. Right before dark we decided to try one last spot. I cut a few times, then yelped, and a turkey gobbled at us. (Stay in the fall woods long enough and you will hear a few gobbles in the fall.)

I cut back a reply and we heard the bird cutting and moving closer. The next time I called, flocks of turkeys opened up on each side of us and started coming in. There were turkeys of all sizes coming in from three directions. Mark ended up taking a nice eastern.

Scatter and Recall

Even though scattering a flock is a less desirable method for me, it's a technique that can't be overlooked. I've used the scatter method when a shot has been missed, when the birds hang up at the fringe of range, or when I can hear another hunter coming into my location. I scare them more for safety's sake than for greed.

The key to a good scatter is to get the birds to go in different directions. To do that you really have to surprise them. I've heard some hunters talk about running at a flock while firing their guns and yelling. That sounds like a heck of an easy way to get yourself hurt or killed.

It's far safer, and just as effective, to carefully lay your gun down, then rush the flock barking like a dog, clapping your hands, or making some other commotion. Try to get as close to the center of the flock as possible and watch to see where the birds go.

If you're working a group of hens and poults, the easiest tactic is to set up at the scatter point. If you think you can get between some of the birds and the scatter point without spooking them, it might be worth a try. The closer you can get, the less that can go wrong.

I usually don't start calling until the turkeys begin trying to regroup. Sometimes the scattered birds will start calling to regroup within a couple of minutes, but sometimes they don't call for an hour. If the woods are fairly open and they can see well, they may regroup by sight and you'll be out of luck. It's even more disheartening when a scattered flock flies to open pastures.

Once you get a bird to call you can usually imitate him, only making the sound more pleading. If you're working young birds you can do well with the kee-kee, and you can often get by just whistling it. If you want to use hen yelps, try a long, lingering, lost call of twenty to thirty yelps.

And speaking of hens, I often ask the people that hunt with me not to shoot the brood hen, so that she can help the brood until spring. She may even pull off another clutch. Then again I don't want that same hen calling all of the poults away from me. If she were to show up again I'd run out and spook her off.

For any number of reasons, a hunter may want to keep scattering a flock. One time a friend and I worked a big mixed flock into bow range and each took three shots. Then we rushed out to flush the birds and retrieve our arrows.

We set back up, waited a while, then called some of the birds back in. This time we shot all of our arrows and flushed the birds again. This went on for the better part of the afternoon until we were totally out of arrows. I did manage to hit a couple of pretty nice trees, and my buddy brought back some feathers from the racing stripe that he shaved across the back of a young gobbler.

There have also been times when I've scattered a flock, then gone to get a friend or another client so he could fill a tag as well. Remember the flock of twenty-five that I tracked and then called in? I brought two more friends to the place where we'd killed the young tom and called in a scattered bird for each of them.

But always remember that scattering a flock of turkeys can lead to an uncertain situation. I've pulled off perfect scatters at first light, then never heard a peep from the birds. I've also rushed in only to have the entire flock flush and head in the same direction.

Without a doubt the best and most successful scattering occurs when you can scare a flock off a roost late in the evening. You can often get close and send them in all different directions. After spending a night by itself on a limb, most turkeys will be more than anxious to regroup at first light.

A few years ago Mike Pearce came over to Missouri for 2½ days of fall hunting. We spent the first two days concentrating on longbeards, working several birds but always encountering one small mishap or another.

As we returned to the house that second evening, my brother Marty was just getting back from a hunt. He'd played with a mixed flock for an hour or more, passing up a bunch of shots at hens and young birds but not quite getting the one longbeard within range.

Knowing that Mike and I would be hunting the next morning he listened for the flock to fly up to roost, then scattered them. Back at the house he described where the birds had been roosted and where they'd flown so that we could go back the next morning.

The scheme worked like a charm. Mike and I slipped to the scattering point just before first light and the turkeys were already calling. Soon it sounded as if we were set up in the middle of a turkey farm. There were purrs, clucks, yelps, cuts, and even an occasional adolescent gobble sounding from all around us.

All it took was a little lost-hen calling. The birds started flying down all around us. More excited hen calls with a few kee-kees tossed in had the birds calling and coming from all directions.

Mike had set his mind on taking the first turkey that came by. He dropped a young bird coming in with a mature hen. He didn't know it, but the longbeard wasn't far behind.

Fall Gobblers

I've saved the best of the fall season for last: hunting fall gobblers. For years people claimed that hunters had to ambush or simply luck onto an autumn longbeard. Some said it was impossible to call in gobblers that were lacking the passion of the mating season. Fortunately gobblers couldn't read this nonsense.

Just such a magazine article was on the newsstands when I entered the woods early one October morning a few years ago. I headed to a place where I'd scouted a nice bachelor flock of longbeards. Like clockwork, at the first hints of daylight I heard the birds' soft talk from a roost near the edge of a big Ozark hollow.

I set up and waited a few minutes before calling to them. They answered back with some yelps and cuts, and I called again. The birds flew down to my right and started excited clucking as soon as their feet hit the leaves. One series of aggressive gobbler yelps had them on their way.

Resting on one knee with big hickories at my front and rear, I faced a large blowdown about ten yards in front of me and a slight break in the hill an equal distance beyond that. I could occasionally glimpse the tops of the toms' heads as they came. I could hear their yelps and cuts almost nonstop. I matched them call for call until they were just beyond the break, when I shut up and got ready.

The birds purred and clucked as they moved up an old trail that passed in front of the blowdown. I drew my bow when all three toms were behind the brush and released an arrow into the tom that walked into the clear first. He weighed twenty pounds and had a ten-inch beard.

There are no real secrets to calling fall gobblers. The basics are the same as calling young birds or hens. Call gobbler to gobbler and try to break into the existing pecking order as the cocky new kid on the block.

Get a bird to respond, imitate his calls with a little more intensity to get him fired up, and you may see things some turkey hunters never

It is not unusual to see some displaying in the autumn due to the pecking order of wild turkeys. You can use their determination of dominance in the pecking order to your advantage in challenging and calling the adult fall gobbler. *Photo by Ray Eye.*

expect to see in the fall. I've heard some excited turkeys gobble once and others gobble every step of the way, just as they do in spring.

It's even more common to see toms strutting as they broadcast their roles in the pecking order. Over the years I've seen fall turkeys get so excited that they break into a fight.

Remember that gobblers usually call a little more slowly and deeply than hens. A good slate call can be tough to beat for gobbler purrs, putts, and cuts. If you like a mouth call, try something raspy like a split-reed diaphragm.

As you've already read, working gobblers on the roost can be extremely effective but you can also do well by moving and calling. I seldom intentionally scatter a bachelor flock of fall gobblers. I've often had pretty poor success getting them to regroup in the near future.

Even when you prefer a big bird, don't pass up the chance to work any bird that will answer a call. It's not uncommon to happen upon a mixed flock that has a longbeard or two in its midst.

You can also use hens and poults to your advantage in getting a gobbler flock to respond. Several times I've been playing with a hen and her brood, getting them all fired up, and a gobbler flock has come running in to see what all of the commotion is about.

The most important tools are confidence and patience. You don't need to be a pro. Over the years I've talked a lot of doubters into trying fall hunts, and quite a few of them have called in and scored on a gobbler during their first season. For some, success came remarkably quickly.

The first time Mike Pearce and I fall hunted together I did all of the calling all morning, but we split to cover more ground that afternoon. Just before we parted, I showed Mike a few important calls and sent him down a promising ridge.

At his first calling site, a bird answered Mike with a few soft yelps. Mike yelped back with a little more feeling. A little later the bird yelped back, and the conversation continued until the longbeard was within twenty feet.

Even if it takes you some time to call in a fall gobbler, stick with it. Sooner or later you'll be sitting in the frosty, full-colored woods with your heart in your throat as you watch a gobbler flock so excited that the birds are shoving each other back and forth as they come.

Experience it once and you'll be hooked for life. That's one of turkey hunting's few certainties.

22

Bowhunting

It was late fall and the turkeys had already settled into their winter pattern. A mixed flock of about forty poults, hens, jakes, and some monster gobblers was roosting at the top of a long, wide Ozark hollow night after night.

Shortly after sunrise they'd fly down, head down the hollow, and cross a little stream to feed in a cut bean field. My brother Marty and I had set up about fifty yards apart halfway down the hollow that morning.

The birds woke up talking and we helped to fuel their fire with our own yelps and excited cutting. For a while they pitched from the trees a bird or two at a time. The last half of the flock left as one, filling the air with the sound of wingbeats and excited calls.

Marty, a champion caller, poured it on the birds while I sat back and listened. I can shut my eyes and still hear the noise. Marty was calling from an old, blown-down cedar and the birds were answering from up the hill.

You didn't have to be an experienced turkey hunter to know that the turkeys were closing in on Marty. Their calls echoed through the hollow, as did the sound of close to eighty feet hustling through the carpet of brittle leaves.

The suspense kept building and building. Finally I could tell that the

Taking a turkey with a bow is one of the biggest challenges in all of hunting. Ray likes to set up with a big tree at his front and rear. *Photo by Mike Pearce.*

turkeys were literally swarming all around Marty, yelping, cutting, clucking, and even occasionally gobbling.

Then came much different sounds: twang, . . . ping, ping, bang, ping, WHACK, followed by even more excited turkey calls. Then twang, . . . ping, ping, bang, ping, WHACK! Next came the roar of wingbeats. Seconds after they faded the sound of soft profanity came from Marty's cedar.

When I walked over I found Marty, knife in hand, trying to cut a broadhead out of an old oak and muttering some unkind words about turkeys. The flock had surrounded him, from poults on up to old gobblers. During the gun season one of the big old boys would have been flopping in the leaves. Since it was bow season all Marty had was a couple of "almosts," one very nice oak, and an unforgettable memory.

So it goes with bowhunting for turkeys.

Each year more and more states offer hunters special archery turkey seasons. Most take place in the fall and run for several weeks, sometimes as long as three months. The bowhunter can take any bird.

There can also be some good bowhunting during the spring season. The spring seasons aren't usually as lengthy and are for gobblers only, but they do have their advantages. For one thing there is usually more foliage in spring to help the hunter get a shot. And then the birds themselves are strutting, gobbling, and carrying on. If you think the hunt is exciting with a gun you ought to try it with a bow.

A hunter who knows what he's doing can squeeze in a lot of fun during the spring and fall seasons. With much skill and an equal amount of luck he may carry home one of the most coveted prizes in bowhunting.

The first thing a new bowhunter has to realize is the difference between gun and bowhunting. Getting the bird up close is the toughest part when you're hunting with a scattergun. It's just half of the battle when you're using a couple of sticks and a string.

You simply can't get good shots off at every bird that comes into range; so you need lots of chances. That's why I suggest most newcomers to the sport look to the fall season — the later the better.

In most areas you'll find turkeys concentrated at one major food source, following somewhat regular patterns. They'll usually roost in one general area and follow the same basic path to food day after day. The birds respond well to calls. You'll usually see several once you find their wintering grounds.

Once you're familiar with their pattern it's time to start looking for a good calling site within their territory. The hardest part of getting a bowshot at a turkey is simply drawing your bow. Unless everything is just right they see the motion and spook.

Finding a good calling position is the most important factor in hunting wild turkeys with a bow and arrow, because you must be able to raise and draw your bow without being seen. *Photo by Ray Eye.*

Some hunters like to use some sort of a blind, but I prefer to be able to move quickly when necessary. I use the terrain to mask my draw.

For instance, as when gun hunting I like to set up with a ridge or break a short distance in front of me. But I also like to have a blowdown, brush pile, or some big cedars between me and the break in the hill.

Since shooting from a sitting position can be difficult with a bow, I like to rest on one knee with the bow vertical in front of me. I consider the tree in front of me more important than the tree at my back. By leaning a bit I can use this tree to block me from the bird's sight. Another tree close behind me to break my outline would be additional insurance.

One of the most important elements in taking a wild turkey with a bow is learning when to make your move, then making it quickly. Personally, I instinctively shoot a recurve bow, which doesn't take long. If you shoot a bow with sights, practice coming to full draw and releasing in one fluid motion.

Common sense says that you never draw on a wild turkey when you can see his head and neck, because he'll see you and spook. I wait until he's behind that blowdown or big cedar in front of me, then make my move just before he steps back out into the open.

Blending in with surroundings is essential. Using a break in the hill or a bend in the edge of a field can help you get a turkey within bow range. *Photo by Ray Eye.*

When drawing your bow, try to wait until the turkey goes behind a tree, blowdown, or some other natural obstacle. It is important when you have your shot to pull and shoot in one fluid movement. *Photo by Ray Eye.*

Putting the shot where it needs to go can also be plenty challenging. Turkeys have a habit of taking an extra step about the time the bowstring slips from your fingers. Even when they're standing stone still you have to hit them in the right place. The closer they are, the easier that is. I never shoot at a turkey with a bow if he's over twenty yards away and I prefer them at twenty feet.

As with deer, I try to put my arrow right in their vitals. The turkey facing away from me offers my favorite shot because everything is so easy to see. Put an arrow through the upper part of the bird's back and you've struck home.

A bird that's walking straight at you offers a good shot as well. If it's a gobbler, try to put the arrow right where the beard enters the body. If it's a hen or a poult, improvise. Be sure you keep your shots high and forward if the bird is standing sideways.

There are many theories about what makes the best turkey hunting arrow. I shoot the same thing I use for deer: a big three- or four-bladed broadhead. Its cutting edge is wide and I can usually put it right where I want it. I'm convinced that accuracy is the key. Of the dozen or so gob-

Arrow placement is essential in harvesting a gobbler with a bow. The vital area of a gobbler is shown from the side. *Photo by Ray Eye.*

A front view of the vital area. Another good shot is the top of the back when the bird is facing away from you. *Photo by Ray Eye.*

blers I've shot through the heart/lung/liver region, very few have done more than thrash after the shot.

Every year I hear stories about people not recovering turkeys shot with arrows. I've heard others talk about following their string-trackers for long distances before finding the crippled bird. Sometimes the loss can't be helped; sometimes it can.

It's my guess that a lot of these birds are hit improperly, many at long ranges. Keep your shots close for better accuracy and also for better access to the bird when necessary.

There are no set rules for what to do after you shoot a turkey with an arrow. If the bird is close and flopping hard, I rush him, put my foot on his neck, and then either wait until he stops thrashing or administer a humane kill.

Play it by ear. If you hit a bird and he jumps up and starts running, you have to decide if you can get to him or if doing so would just spook him even more. You also have to consider how safe it is to go running

A good rule of thumb is, if you don't have a good shot, just don't shoot. Photo by Ray Eye.

through the woods after a turkey that may have a razor-sharp broadhead sticking out of his body.

If you have a string-tracker, make sure the line is flowing smoothly and let it do the work. If you don't have a string-tracker, use your ears and eyes to figure out where the wounded bird is headed.

As with deer, don't be in a big hurry to find a wounded turkey that's run off. Check the ground for tiny drops of blood and a trail of feathers. There usually won't be much to follow; so pay close attention.

If the bird's hit hard, it will probably head downhill and might well try to hole up in the thickest cover around. Check deep within brush piles, blowdowns, undercut banks and the like. Make a thorough search for a well-shot turkey and you'll probably find it.

But more than likely, finding errant arrows will consume more of your time than looking for hit turkeys. You'll also spend more time talking about the shots that you almost had instead of the ones you had.

There are a seemingly infinite number of things that can go wrong when you're bowhunting for turkeys. Even the most well-planned hunts can fall to pieces in a hurry. Then again, sooner or later the odds will change.

The hunt with my two friends was an impulsive idea. I wasn't really ready when they showed up and I wasn't as prepared as I like to be when we walked into the woods.

After a while we split up to cover three separate ridges. We hadn't been apart long when a bird yelped a response to my calls. The bird was close, just over the lip of a ridge. It couldn't have been sixty yards away.

As luck would have it, I was set up in a perfect calling site with a little ravine in front of me and a scattering of cedars all around.

I let out a few more fall calls that were met by excited clucks. Countering with some cutting I could hear the birds moving my way.

My heart went into overdrive when five longbeards came trotting over the ridge in a tight little group. They never broke stride as they dropped down into the ravine.

When they were all out of sight I raised my bow and got it to full draw just as the lead bird stepped up into sight. With his head and neck behind a cedar and the rest of his body totally exposed, he stopped, barely fifteen feet away. The arrow seemed to release itself and smacked the bird right where it was supposed to.

The time between when I first heard the toms to when I stood over one couldn't have been more than a couple of minutes. It was my best bird with a bow: 22½ pounds, long spurs, and a bushy 11-inch beard.

I know I'll probably never bow-kill another bird to top that one. But I'll keep trying, and I'll keep missing shots and spooking turkeys when I'm trying to draw. It will still be lots of fun, and after all, fun is what turkey hunting is all about. The kill, especially the killing of a trophy bird, is just a bonus.

23

Equipment

Even though your scouting told you he'd probably be there, the turkey's gobbling at your first crow call still catches you a little off guard. After taking a few seconds to pour over your mental map of the area, you head to a little clearing on the tom's level. There are no obstacles between the gobbler and you, only open woods and the remnants of an old two-track road.

With a slight ridge thirty yards in front of you, you nestle into the base of a big oak, drop a headnet over your face, rest the gun on your knees, and cut loose with some soft yelps. The bird gobbles back an immediate reply.

Thirty minutes later the conversation is still going on. The bird, probably a veteran of four or five spring seasons, has showed some hesitation, but well-timed cutting has brought him to just beyond the rise.

He's close enough that you can easily hear him spitting and drumming. His last gobble is loud enough that you actually feel it, as well as hear it. You give a couple of soft, soothing purrs and you can see just the top of a fanned tail slowly moving toward you.

Seconds later the entire bird is in sight, almost glowing in the early morning light. For an instant or two you're almost spellbound by the bird's beauty and size. Another thundering gobble snaps you back to reality. You encircle the trigger of your shotgun with a quivering finger and start to pull.

The real work—getting a mature gobbler to come that close—is behind you. The hunt is already an overwhelming success (at least in my opinion), but what happens next will determine whether the tom will become the icing on an already unforgettable cake.

The concept is very simple: you need something that will travel from you to the turkey with enough shock to turn off his central nervous system. That's not that difficult with the right kind of gun and ammunition.

Turkey Guns

In some states it's legal to shoot a turkey with a center-fire rifle. But since I have no experience, nor plan on ever getting any experience shooting a turkey with a rifle, I don't feel qualified to write about the subject.

As you may have already read, I shot my first turkey with an old Winchester Model 97 12-gauge pumpgun. If you'd asked me then, I'd have sworn that such a gun was the best, if the not the only, gun for turkey hunting.

Since then I've seen gobblers shot with $20,000 custom guns and with old hand-me-downs held together simply by a combination of rust, electrician's tape, and a pair of strong hands. I'm convinced there is no one shotgun that does *the* best job of killing a turkey. There are an abundance of guns that will do the job. You have to decide which is right for you.

For the past ten to fifteen years the trend has been toward bigger when it comes to turkey guns. There's no doubt that a big 10-gauge or a 12-gauge full of three-inch Magnums can make a heck of a turkey gun, but this tendency can be taken a little too far.

Back in the 1970s some friends and I got together to do some target shooting and check out the new shotguns some of my buddies had just bought for turkey hunting. The guns were three-inch, 12-gauge Magnums with barrels that seemed as long as broom handles.

At first my friends started shooting at tin cans about forty yards away, and soon they were taking shots at sixty and seventy yards, then even further. After each shot they'd rush out to count the few pellet holes in 12-ounce cans. After finding four or five holes following a seventy-yard shot one of my friends said something like "... there ain't going to be a turkey safe in the woods."

Setting up a can at about sixty yards, he turned to me and said, "Hey Ray, get your old gun and see what it'll do at that range." I knew they

Equipment

were kidding me about my old square-back Browning 12-gauge that only shot 2¾-inch shells.

At the time it was the gun I used for everything. I loaded it with No. 8 shot for quail and slugs for deer and I killed quite a few turkeys with it.

I stood there and listened to my friends teasing me and insulting my gun for a while before picking up the old Browning and sliding a shell in the chamber. Standing beside my friends, I raised the gun, aimed at the far-off dot of a can and pushed off the safety. Then I quickly lowered the muzzle and blew a plate-sized hole in the dirt about twenty steps away. "See that," I said, "I've never shot a turkey much farther away than that. I can get by with what I already have."

From what I've seen, some people buy a 10-gauge or big Magnum 12-gauge for all of the wrong reasons. Armed with the most powerful shotgun in America they seem to think they can pull off superhuman shots. The result is many more wounded turkeys in the woods. To me, that's not what turkey hunting is all about.

Sure, I shoot a 12-gauge Magnum now but my philosophy about range has never changed. The most important part about shooting a turkey is getting him in close for positive identification and a clean kill.

But there are some big advantages to the larger shotguns if you use them for added insurance rather than long-range artillery. The shells you shoot carry more pellets and deliver a real knock-out punch when used properly.

Then again, they also have their disadvantages. For one thing, they can be pretty heavy. The extra weight may not feel like much when you're carrying it from the gun case to the car, but put in six or eight miles in rugged terrain and it may seem as if you're lugging a cannon.

The guns can also have a punishing recoil and muzzle-blast that might bother some people. Wearing a good set of hearing protectors when you're shooting targets can make a Magnum shotgun much more tolerable. If you don't like the kick, then step down to a smaller gun. You can't shoot accurately if you're wincing and blinking like a toad in a hail storm when you pull the trigger.

A good test to see if you're a little shy of a big gun is to grab a friend and go to a shooting range. Face the other way while your friend handles the loading. Sometime during the shoot have him leave the chamber empty. If you catch yourself wincing after the hammer falls, you know you're probably flinching on live shells as well. It's a little embarrassing to make this discovery in front of a friend, but you'll feel even worse if you cripple a gobbler or two.

There's nothing wrong with using a regular 12-gauge or even a 16- or a 20-gauge if you load it properly, know its limitations, and don't take marginal shots. I'll discuss how to get the most out of the smaller gauges a little later.

One of the most important parts of a shotgun is the last few inches of the barrel where it's choked. If you have a gun with changeable chokes, use the tightest choke possible. The best way to take a tom is to center the densest possible pattern of shot on his head and neck.

A full or even an extra-full choke is the hands-down favorite for most turkey hunters. A modified choke will work as a second choice if you use special loads and keep the shots close. Hunters whose guns have the more open chokes may want to consider purchasing another barrel, getting a choke system installed, or even buying another gun.

If you are in the market for a new shotgun, the length of the barrel might be a prime consideration. Up until a few years ago it was widely believed that the longer the barrel the tighter the pattern. While this concept sounds reasonable, tests have shown barrel lengths to have little effect on pattern.

The shorter barrels, say, from twenty-three to twenty-six inches have several advantages over longer lengths. One obvious plus is a slight reduction in weight. Another is handling ease; a barrel that's two feet long takes a lot less time and effort to swing and aim than one that's a full yard long.

Since turkey guns are aimed rather than pointed, as on an upland bird hunt, a large front bead can be a big plus. A good gunsmith can install such a sight onto a beadless barrel for a small fee. Some hunters even add standard rifle sights to their turkey guns.

Shotgun action is largely a matter of hunter preference. Almost every action has its share of advantages and disadvantages. A single-shot shotgun is as light as possible and is the cheapest shotgun made. My brother Marty had good success with an old single-shot for years.

But the only problem with a single-shot is clear from its name—you get only a single shot. Done properly, turkey hunting should boil down to one good shot. It's nice, though, to have a follow-up shot at a wounded bird if needed.

Some people like the fine balance and looks of a side-by-side or double-barrel, but their prices can be more than many hunters are willing to spend.

A semiautomatic can offer fast and accurate follow-up shots if needed and a slightly reduced recoil. But on rare occasions they can jam up. The pump shotgun has probably the most versatile action on any gun. Some models sell for very reasonable prices, with the only real drawback being the effort needed to pump a shell from the magazine into the chamber.

Many of today's special turkey guns come with a dull finish to eliminate the problem of a shiny surface spooking a nearby gobbler.

Equipment 173

Shotguns with the standard bluing and glossy wood can either be painted or covered with camouflage tape or elastic sock.

A sling can be a great investment, making the shotgun easier to haul and freeing your hands to carry calls, cameras, and perhaps a dead turkey.

Even though shooting a turkey might seem pretty easy, there's always room for practice. Spend some time handling your turkey gun before each season. Make sure you've handled the gun enough that it comes up smoothly and that your head just naturally nestles into the stock.

It's also good to head to the woods to practice shooting from a sitting position. And while you're at it, practice taking some shots from your off shoulder. Sooner or later every right-handed shooter is challenged with a bird coming in on his right.

It's much easier to simply move the gun butt a few inches rather than try to scoot your whole body around to take the shot. I've taken at least a half-dozen toms shooting left-handed.

Another little trick that can make a difference is learning how to quietly slip your gun's safety off by sliding it easily between your thumb and forefinger.

Turkey Ammunition

Guns and ammunition are a lot like a hunter and his dog: the little one does most of the work and the big one gets all of the credit. The shells you choose can make or break a hunt.

First you need to rule out using the really big shot sizes, such as No. 2s and buckshot on turkeys. The pellets may hit harder than smaller shot, but they're so few in number that the pattern is far too sparse to make consistent head and neck shots on a turkey. The large shot sizes are also far more dangerous for hunters.

And forget about using those huge loads for body shots. Trying to get a few pellets through a big gobbler's wings, feathers, breast, and breast sponge and into a bird's vitals is all but impossible.

I've seen turkeys either run or fly off after being literally knocked off their feet by a body shot with goose loads. A friend once took a nice Merriam gobbler that had two dozen No. 2 pellets buried in its breast and thighs. Had he not killed the tom just a few days after it was wounded it would have faced a long and painful death. No turkey deserves such an end.

Shot sizes 4 through 7½ are the best to choose, with 4s and 6s being the most popular. I've always had the best success with 6s but some of my peers swear by 4s.

Use of shells loaded with 7½ shot seems to be increasing. That makes sense if you're after a dense pattern. After all, there are well over twice as many pellets in a load of 7½s as compared to No. 4 shot.

The main question is whether shot that small will retain enough energy to penetrate a tom's neck or skull. The answer is yes; at normal turkey hunting ranges 7½ shot performs very well. Ben "Bear" Held, a good friend of mine, has been using nothing else for years, and he's built up a pretty impressive record.

Those who shoot a relatively small gun, or a gun with a modified choke, may want to take a hard look at the smaller pellets like 6s or 7½s. A standard 12-gauge shell loaded with 6s will have more pellets than a three-inch shell of 4s. Any added pellets can also help to fill in the holes left by a modified choke.

Shotgun pellet construction can help determine how a particular load will perform. Extra-hard pellets will not only have more impact, they'll also fly truer because they won't become misshapen from the pressure of sitting in the wad and the shot. Most quality loads feature pellets that have been copper- or nickel-plated for added hardness.

Plastic granules in the shot column can be another bonus for dense patterns. The tiny specks of plastic fill in between the pellets, keeping them from knocking into each other and dispersing the pattern in early flight.

Shooting a buffered load of quality shot is almost like changing to the next tightest choke at most turkey hunting ranges. That's something good to know if you're carrying a gun with a modified choke.

It's also worth mentioning that some hunters have been using steel shot to get tighter patterns. The down-range slowness and comparatively light weight of steel pellets make it imperative to keep your shots close, but that's the name of the game anyway.

Generally speaking, the more powder, the better for down-range penetration. There is, however, such a thing as too much powder, which brings us to the most important concept of guns and ammunition: patterning to discover what load provides the densest pattern in your gun.

Sometimes shells crammed full of powder and pellets don't pattern well. The only way you're going to know is to shoot a few shells at paper to check for pattern density.

Try as many different shells as possible to see which works best from your gun. Trading a few shells with other hunters is a good way to cut down on the costs of experimentation.

Don't make the mistake of not being critical enough when you're patterning a load and gun. Forget about all of the skin, flesh, and wattles on a turkey. What you're aiming at, the brain and neckbone, isn't much bigger than a piece of licorice with a big marshmallow on top.

Most state wildlife departments offer patterning sheets that feature

Equipment

an x-ray view of a turkey's head and neck so that you'll know exactly where your pellets are hitting. Ask around. Many avid turkey hunters keep extra copies on hand.

Start off by patterning your gun at close range, like ten to fifteen yards. Then move back in five-yard increments. You'll eventually find your gun's maximum range. Remember what it is and never, never shoot any farther. No matter what the patterning sheets tell me, I never shoot over thirty-five to forty yards.

How many pellets need to strike home for the load to be good enough for hunting? Even though usually "it only takes one," I believe you need at least a dozen to insure clean kills time after time.

Once you've decided on a good load, use it as often as possible to instill confidence. Knowing that your gun/load combination can, and will, take down a gobbler will give you one less concern and slightly steadier nerves when the moment arrives.

Pattern your gun often and use the load in your turkey gun to do such things as shoot clay targets or simple plinking. I'll never forget the first time that I shot the federal load of two ounces of No. 6 shot through my Remington 1100 SP Magnum.

Mike Pearce and I had met to work on a project. Taking an afternoon break, Mike got out a box of the then new two-ounce loads and I pulled out "Maggie."

We had no patterning paper, and so I stuck a soda can against a tall creek bank twenty yards away. I slipped one of the heavy shells into the chamber, rested the gun against a tree, and squeezed the trigger. My ears rang and my shoulder snapped back from the recoil.

But all of the discomfort vanished when I looked at the can. It was literally demolished, looking as if it had been hit with a lawn mower. I put the gun on paper a few days later and it looked as if the target had been forced through the bottom of a sieve.

When I take a bead on a gobbler's neck at twenty to thirty yards I know exactly what's going to happen. If I do my part the gun and load will do theirs. That peace of mind more than makes up for the noise and the recoil.

Archery Equipment

Taking a big game animal with a bow and calling a turkey in so close that you can see the light in his coal-black eyes and the creases between the wrinkles on his head are two of the greatest challenges in hunting. Combine them and you have possibly the greatest accomplishment in the sport.

When a hunter uses a gun to take a turkey, the shot itself is some-

This hunter has chosen a recurve hunting bow for hunting turkeys. The most important thing is that a hunter is familiar with his equipment, knows its capabilities, and has confidence in it. *Photo by Ray Eye.*

what anticlimactic. The hardest part is simply getting the bird within range. After that you try to center his head and neck in something about the size of a dinner plate.

But when you shoot with a bow, you use something that's usually less than two inches wide to hit a target that's not much bigger. Making the shot is half of the battle. Consequently, there's no room for anything but the best equipment.

I've shot several turkeys with an old fifty-pound recurve and always felt it was more than strong enough. But there are some advantages to shooting a bow with a strong draw weight. It can help provide the most important element—accuracy. The flatter your bow shoots the better, whether that's accomplished with stronger limbs, cams, or whatever.

Whether the hunter shoots a compound or a recurve bow with a glove or a release is again up to the shooter. But I really can't overemphasize the need for the greatest accuracy. Hitting a turkey in the wrong place usually means a lost turkey. Sometimes the bird may go a long time before dying.

Terry Funk, Kansas Department of Wildlife and Parks Turkey Project Leader, often tells of a big Rio Grande gobbler that lasted months with an aluminum arrow sticking out both sides of his breast. His condition was so bad that the bird had trouble getting his wings fully closed. The hunter missed his mark by maybe six inches, but the result was still a badly wounded bird.

The main idea is to shoot a bow smoothly and comfortably. Don't use equipment if you have to give a hard yank to get to full draw. Because of the difficulty in drawing on a close bird, you'll want a bow that you can quickly and smoothly pull straight back to your anchor point.

There really isn't any need for a special turkey bow. If you're already bowhunting for deer, your current outfit will do fine. If you are thinking about getting a new bow, you may want to look into one of the shorter models, which would be less conspicuous and easier to handle when making your move on a turkey.

Probably more important than the type or weight of your bow are the little things that you do to it. For one thing, you don't want even the slightest noise when making a draw. The same goes for noise at the shot. A good pro shop can show you a variety of ways to prevent such problems.

You'll also want to keep the bow tuned so that it provides the greatest accuracy. That means having the limbs set the same. If your bow is adjustable, find out what weight produces the tightest groups.

How you camouflage a bow is largely a matter of personal preference. Many avid bowhunters carry painted bows but some use easily removable tape. No matter what you use, see how it affects your accuracy.

Arrows should match your draw length and draw weight perfectly for optimum accuracy. Aluminum is the hands-down favorite for a flat trajectory and good penetration. Plastic vanes for fletching have the advantage of being waterproof, but many archers still carry arrows fletched with feathers, claiming the natural material gives them better accuracy. Again, if you're new to archery, a good pro shop can save you a lot of time and money finding what's right for you and your bow.

Personally, I've always liked my arrows tipped with accurate, razor-sharp broadheads. The more cutting edge, the better, as long as they fly well time after time.

There seems to be an almost endless variety of specialty products designed for archery turkey hunting. I tend to avoid most, but that decision rests with the shooter.

Some hunters put little washerlike stoppers on their arrows to keep them from achieving full penetration. The concept is that a turkey couldn't escape as easily with thirty inches of arrow sticking from him. Some claim that the washer also provides added shock.

Using a string tracker is another popular alternative. It's simply a highly visible thread that's fastened to the arrow and attached to a spool that sits on the bow. If all goes as planned, you just follow the string to the turkey, unless he died in his tracks or flew off.

The main problems with arrow-stoppers and string-trackers are the effect they might have on accuracy and the inconvenience of using them. More than one hunter has gotten the thread on his string-tracker tangled, causing a shot to fly off the mark.

But if you have the money and the interest to try such things, by all means take them to the range. But don't give up even a fraction of an inch of accuracy for a little gadgetry. If you do opt for something like a string-tracker, be willing to put in the pre-season hours necessary to make using it seem second nature. If you have the confidence that it works for you, chances are it will.

There's no such thing as too much shooting practice before you try to take a turkey with a bow. The vital heart/lung area, which is where I always aim, on even a mature gobbler is not much bigger than a grapefruit. You have to be both accurate and confident.

Start off shooting at very close distances, like five yards, and gradually move back. When you get to the distance at which you can't put four out of five arrows into an area the size of your fist, you're past your maximum hunting range. Few good turkey hunters will try a bow shot past twenty yards.

Since a turkey's kill zone is totally unlike that of most big game, it doesn't hurt to buy some targets that outline the chest cavity. If you can't find those, draw your own targets and aim for where the wings enter the body.

If you're new to hunting turkeys with a bow, try to learn as much as possible about the anatomy of a bird. Look at some dressed birds to see where the vital organs are located, then try to visualize them on every turkey photo you see.

Try to spend as much time as possible shooting under realistic conditions. Shooting judo-points in the woods at unmarked yardages while wearing your full hunting outfit can be excellent practice.

Practice from both the kneeling and standing positions. If you can figure out a way to do it when hunting, try taking shots from a sitting position as well. If you're going to be hunting from a blind of some sort, then practice shooting from it religiously.

There's one thing you can't practice for, though: how you're going to handle the excitement you feel when that big bird steps up and your bow is drawn. That's a bridge you have to cross when you come to it.

It will sure be a whole lot easier to reach the other side of that bridge if you know you're shooting good equipment very, very well.

Hunting Clothes

After calls and guns, good camouflage can be a turkey hunter's most important equipment. Hunting turkeys is a game of getting an alert bird with razor-sharp eyes into close range. Good camouflage can make that much easier to accomplish.

My tastes in camouflage have changed a lot since I was a teenager. Back then "camo" meant a ratty old camouflage jacket, a matching hat, and a pair of faded overalls. Of course there was more available, but getting it took money, getting money meant a job, and getting a job meant less time for calling turkeys. That idea never lasted very long.

So I made do with what I had, using good calling positions and the ability to hold stone still for whatever length of time it took to get a gobbler up close. The approach worked for me then, and it would work for me now if I gave it a chance.

But there's simply too much good camouflage on the market at affordable prices to excuse being any less than totally prepared. Hunters shooting other hunters in the woods every spring is an added incentive: when some fool starts stalking my turkey calls I want to be as invisible as possible.

The choices seem almost endless in camouflage clothing. There are more patterns and styles available than most of us ever dreamed of just a few years ago.

While there are a few key industry leaders, there's a place for almost every camouflage on the market. It's up to you to decide which place you're in.

As for camo patterns, just try to find something that matches your hunting location. There are a lot of variations across America. The deep greens and dark browns that work so well in the big woods of Dixie won't blend in on the prairies where lighter browns and similar hues work best.

If you're hunting the traditional hardwoods a camo pattern modeled after the bark of a tree may work well. Rely as much on common sense as on which company spends the most on advertising.

Your decisions are far from over once you've picked a pattern, since there are so many styles and articles of clothing. Obviously the jacket is going to be your number one concern. Be sure you pick out something that's lightweight and quiet. Staying warm isn't usually a problem, but when it is, another layer of clothes or long underwear will do the trick.

Good old cotton and cotton blends are tough to beat. I usually advise staying away from most of the synthetic fabrics. They'll keep you dry but when you move, they often sound like a handful of newspapers being crumpled.

Choose a camouflage pattern that matches the terrain you are hunting. *Photo by Ray Eye.*

It's a good idea to select a jacket that's a little big. Some people buy a full size larger than usual so that they can move comfortably and easily. A larger jacket also allows you to dress for the weather. If it's freezing, there's room for a couple of sweatshirts. When it's hot and muggy, you can get by with just a long-sleeved T-shirt.

As for styles, I like a coat that hangs well below my waist. Additionally, it must, and I mean absolutely must, have plenty of big pockets to accommodate a wide range of calls, shells, and other paraphernalia.

Look for the same basic qualities in a pair of camouflage pants: lots of pockets and enough room for easy movement and comfort.

It sounds a little odd, but you may want to consider pants in a different color and pattern than your hunting coat. I seldom wear a matching coat and pants because the forest floor seldom matches the trees I'm sitting against.

Many times I'll be sitting with my legs surrounded by nothing but dead leaves; so I'll wear pants with a brown leaf pattern. But don't let me make your decision. Think of what it's like where you hunt and dress accordingly.

Personally, I like a baseball-style camouflage hat for turkey hunting. It's inexpensive and fits well, and it has a long bill that can help keep the sun out of your eyes. When pulled down low it also casts a shadow over your face. Normally it's best if the pattern of your hat matches your jacket.

A good pair of camouflaged gloves can help mask any inadvertent hand movement. Hunters can choose the traditional jersey glove in a couple of camouflage patterns as well as gloves made of lightweight mesh.

I tend to opt for the jersey gloves because they fit better. I also like to cut the fingertips off for greater sensitivity when I'm working a call or gun. You'll also discover that cutting the ends off a pair of cotton gloves makes them much more comfortable in warm weather.

Nothing seems to glow in the early morning quite like a pale, uncovered face. Pulling a billed cap down low helps, as does a full beard. It's a combination I've used to call a lot of turkeys to some very close ranges.

But there's no use taking chances when there are so many ways to camouflage your face. Without a doubt the most effective way is with face paints. Dabbing your face with two or three colors that match the surroundings not only helps you blend in, it's also comfortable and does nothing to impair your vision.

There are some disadvantages, however, such as the time it takes to apply and remove the make-up or the remarks you suffer when you go into a public place. It's for that reason that most hunters rely on some sort of headnet or cloth to cover their faces.

A shiny face is a great way to spook a gobbler. Ray likes to use a facenet that's sewn into his cap. He prefers the kind with a hole in the net for his eyes. *Photo by Mike Pearce.*

Equipment

One of the simplest methods is to pull a camouflaged bandana up over your nose bank-robber style. There are also a variety of mesh headnets from which to choose. My favorite comes up to the bridge of my nose, covering my face but not impairing my vision. The hat pulled down low covers my forehead.

Some hunters opt for a headnet that covers the entire head because they think that their eyes should be covered as well. If you take that route be sure to spend a lot of time with the net on your head so that you'll be used to looking through it. But stay out of liquor and convenience stores when you're wearing it.

There are also facenets with pre-cut eyeholes for better visibility. Other good alternatives are the camouflage nets that are attached to the inside of a hunting hat. The nets do a good job of covering the face and neck, and they also store easily within the hat when not in use.

The market has also seen the introduction of several other items to help a hunter blend in, such as small clip-on leaves that hang from the coat or hat to give the camouflage a three-dimensional effect and a bit more realism.

There's actually no end to the lengths that a hunter could go to to make sure he blends into his hunting grounds. Each individual has to decide what he thinks he needs. One Ozark hunter I met was so worried

Shiny gun barrels should be covered with paint, tape, or a slide-on sock such as on this double-barrel. *Photo by Mike Pearce.*

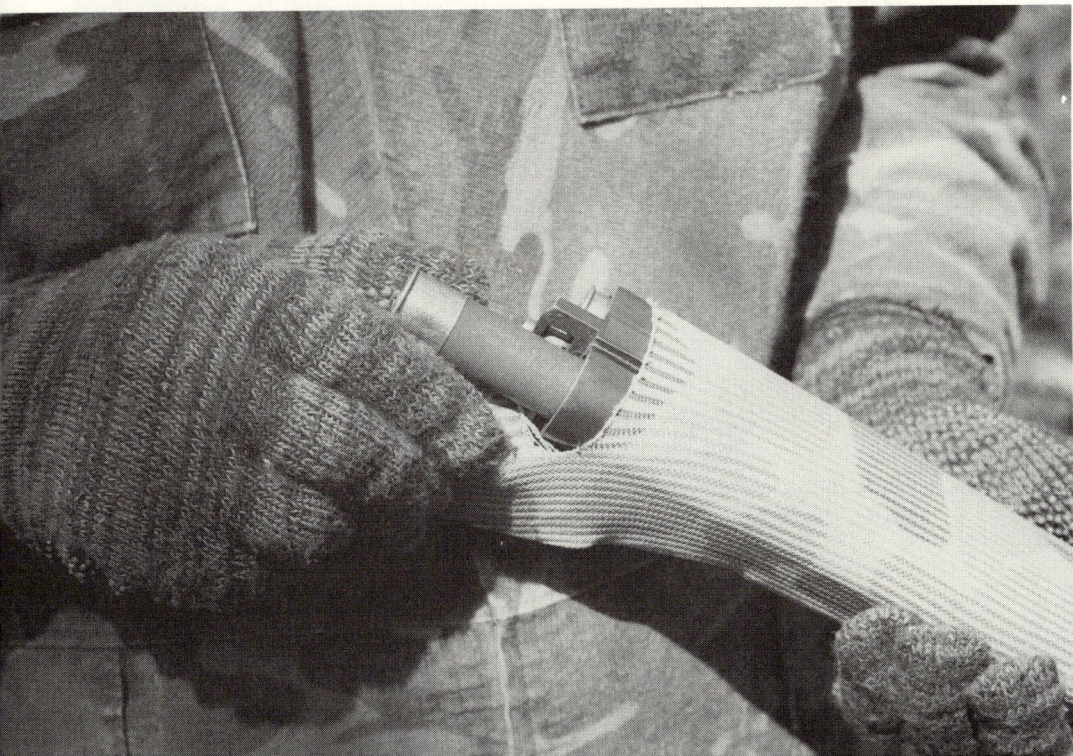

that a turkey would see him smiling that he painted his teeth green, brown, and black. (At least I think it was paint.)

The main idea is to have that ever-important total confidence in what you're wearing. But always remember that good camouflage is an aid and not a cure-all. No matter how well you're dressed, there's no substitute for holding still.

Boots

Wearing the right footwear can do a great deal to improve the success of a turkey hunt. It obviously doesn't have much effect on the birds, but it can determine whether the hunter is comfortable or miserable.

Like clothing, boots are offered in great variety, and no one boot is right for everyone. You need to consider how far you walk, the slope of the terrain, the amount of standing water, and the temperature.

One of the most important considerations is that boots fit correctly and have good ankle support. Since I cover a lot of ground, weight is also a factor. If you're walking five miles a morning, any extra ounces will feel like pounds by the time you leave the woods.

Keeping your feet dry can be difficult whether you're hunting in the dew-soaked grasslands of Kansas or in the swamps of Florida. Materials like Gore-Tex have helped a lot. With proper care, these materials can keep you remarkably comfortable. Still, such boots weren't made for wading or extended standing in water. For that you need rubber. Rubber-bottomed boots with leather uppers still offer some good support. Full-length rubber boots are totally waterproof but aren't the most comfortable for walking.

Turkey hunting in the mountains requires a good pair of boots with non-skid soles. A boot with a waffle-style pattern on Vibram soles allows you to keep your footing where other boots might leave you sliding.

Many boot companies have started producing camouflaged boots. To be honest, there's nothing wrong with the traditional dull browns. Turkeys have actually walked over my leather boots without showing any sign of alarm. But if having camouflaged boots makes you more confident, then by all means wear them.

Accessories

There's almost no end to the list of items that could come in handy on a turkey hunt. I've listed most of the more popular equipment that some people carry. But remember this: if you head into the woods with all of these, you'll be weighed down like an overburdened pack mule.

Equipment

Pack

Personally, I can carry all that I want to take in the pockets of my pants and hunting jacket. The result can be a little bulky but I'm used to it. Some hunters like to stash their gear in a lightweight fanny pack. It's small, rides comfortably, and can give easy access to its contents.

If you decide on a fanny pack, be sure to get one that's made out of a soft and quiet material. It's amazing how much noise something like nylon can make when scraping against trees and brush.

Flashlight

Finding your way into the timber before daylight or leaving after dark can be much easier with a flashlight. Flashlights that use only two AA batteries are small, easy to carry, yet provide enough light for walking down a trail.

Compass

Some people believe carrying a compass is a sign of weakness. The way I see it, there's no strength to be gained from wandering in the wilderness for a couple of days.

I'm fortunate to have a natural sense of direction. But I've hunted with some who could get lost in the bathtub. It never hurts to take a good compass with you and to use a distinguishing landmark as a reference. You not only won't get lost, but you'll also have the confidence to cover more territory. And that often means you'll find more turkeys.

Map

Some hunters carry a small topographical map, especially if they don't know the area well. The maps don't prevent a hunter from getting lost as much as they help him read the lay of the land. For example, if you're on one ridge and hear a tom gobbling somewhere over another, you can check the map to see where the bird might be and how to move in on him.

Binoculars

Quite a few turkey hunters on the plains and in western mountains carry binoculars whenever they hunt. They head for the highest ground and spend some time looking for feeding or displaying turkeys. Once they spot birds they close the distance and start calling.

If you're going to use binoculars be sure to consider their weight and the amount of walking you're going to be doing. Some models are small enough to fit in a shirt pocket and light enough to go unnoticed.

Extra Calls and Materials

This is something of an emergency kit that you carry in the depths of a pocket or pack and never remove until needed. It never hurts to have an old mouth call stashed away in case your old favorite breaks a reed or gets lost somewhere between calling sites.

If you use a friction call, you can never carry along too much box-call chalk or sandpaper for your slate. Sooner or later, you're going to lose one and need the other.

Cushion

Sitting on hard ground and rocks can wear a little heavy on some people's backsides. If you're one of those people, you may want to carry a small foam cushion to make life more bearable. The more comfortable you are, the easier it is to sit perfectly still.

Make sure the material covering the seat blends in well with the surroundings and is relatively quiet. The cushion should also be waterproof for days when the woods are wet.

Knife/Clippers

Most hunters always carry a knife when they enter the woods. I like to carry a small, but sturdy, folding lockblade knife for dressing turkeys and such.

Sometimes a lightweight pair of clippers can come in handy to trim small limbs and branches near your calling sight. Clippers can also enable a hunter to construct a blind much more quickly and quietly.

Camouflage Netting

Speaking of blinds, there are some places in America where good calling sites are few and far between. A line of cottonwoods in a grazed cow pasture would offer little cover for setting up and calling.

Some hunters solve this problem with a small piece of camouflage netting. They drape the netting over a few sticks or bushes for additional cover. It's important that the netting match the surroundings and that it's arranged so that you can still see and shoot over or through it with no difficulty.

Equipment

Insect Repellent

You don't know agony unless you've sat in a swamp in the Deep South, a gobbler slowly approaching while a couple of hundred mosquitoes feast on you. Even if you could move, you couldn't swat them all away, and it doesn't take long for the buzzing to drive you crazy.

At about that time you'd give a day's pay for a little quality insect repellent. In the best brands on the market a substance commonly known as DEET makes up eighty to one hundred percent of the ingredients. Only a few drops on your hands, neck, and face can discourage the likes of chiggers, ticks, and "skeeters." They can make the difference between a hunt you'll always remember and one you'd like to forget.

Rain Gear

Spring not only brings gobbling turkeys, it also carries the threat of rain. Some hunters like to wear a lightweight, camouflaged rain suit when things start getting wet. Finding a rain suit that's quiet, well camouflaged, and comfortable enough for walking mile after mile can be a problem.

I never travel without rain gear but unless there's a real downpour I usually wear my regular camouflage and plan to get wet. If I start to feel miserable, I head to camp for a quick cup of coffee and a dry change of camouflage clothes.

Fluorescent Orange

Ideally we could walk into the woods and totally immerse ourselves in the fun of turkey hunting. But we can't, because doing that might get us hurt, or maybe even killed.

All turkey hunters should take along something that undoubtedly identifies them as human beings, and there's nothing better than something that's colored fluorescent orange. Most sporting goods stores sell inexpensive vests that you can slip on while you're walking and wad into your pocket when you're calling. They're also great for wrapping around a gobbler for the walk back to the vehicle.

Camera

A good camera takes up so little room yet provides so many memories. And there are so many things to be photographed, including sunrises and sunsets, pretty scenery, and special moments. Taking a picture of a bagged gobbler where he falls will always mean more than a posed shot in your garage a couple of hours later.

Hunters can buy a name-brand, automatic 35mm camera for under a hundred dollars these days. Some are even small enough to fit into a shirt pocket.

First Aid Kit

Most avid outdoorsmen carry a small first aid kit in their vehicles. It's also wise to put a few Band-Aids in your pocket for blisters.

Et Cetera

Like many people, I have problems rolling out of bed at 3 A.M. and sitting down to a big breakfast. But by the time the sun's been up an hour or two my stomach starts rumbling even if I ate at camp. Some of the finest breakfasts I've ever tasted have been in the turkey woods while I've been working a bird.

It usually doesn't take much to hold a hunter over until lunch. Some hunters like granola bars or dried fruit mixes. My tastes are a little simpler: a couple of cookies, or better yet, a fried egg and bacon sandwich and an orange.

A small canteen of drinking water or small bottle of juice can also come in handy, since most creek and lake water isn't fit for human consumption.

For those who are interested, here is a list of the equipment I usually take to the woods:

Diaphragm calls
Box and slate calls
Shotgun
Half-dozen shells
Trimmed jersey gloves
Mesh headnet
Folding knife
Small flashlight
Small flask
Fluorescent orange
Occasionally a camera
Usually a snack
Always, always toilet tissue

Decoys

The concept of a turkey decoy is pretty sound: if an approaching gobbler sees something he thinks is a hen, he'll hurry right in. I've never

A decoy can be useful in some situations. Decoy placement is important due to safety factors. Some hunters just don't pay attention and a lot of decoys are shot every year. Always set your decoy in a clearing, never broadside to you as it is in this photo. You need control of the situation so that another hunter cannot approach you without your knowing it. Sometimes gobblers will run to a decoy, other times away from it. *Photo by Ray Eye.*

cared much for using decoys because I put so much emphasis on good calling and good calling position.

If everything went well, the gobbler wouldn't see the decoy until he was twenty yards away, and by then he'd already be in range. I've also found decoys a little bulky and not the safest thing to tuck under your arm when walking through the woods.

But there are people who have had great success with decoys, especially those hunting more open habitats. Full-bodied decoys work best but silhouettes usually get the job done too.

Hunters who are inexperienced with decoys need to pay close attention to decoy placement. Decoys can work for or against you if you place them too far out front. A gobbler may well hang up twenty or thirty yards away from the decoy — or even farther — to display and wait for the hen to make the next move. Try to set the decoy so that the turkey will pass you on his way to the artificial sweetheart.

Use great caution when using a decoy. I recommend that the decoys face directly away from you in a field or clearing so that the full image is at your side. Stay a few trees back in the timber and watch and listen for other hunters sneaking in. Keep the decoy covered or draped in fluorescent orange as you move from place to place.

24

Safety

It all seemed to be so perfect for Arlon Held. He'd located a gobbler and had closed the distance. His calling position was perfect and the bird was fired up and on his way.

Arlon had his gun up and was scanning the woods in front of him for the gobbler that should show up at any second. My good friend was being cautious, moving only his eyes and listening for any telltale hints of the approaching turkey.

But the next sound he heard was far from what he was expecting. A loud roar boomed from his right and his head jerked to the left. Momentarily stunned, he soon figured out what had happened: someone had shot at him. It wasn't an accidental discharge, either. Someone had aimed a gun at him and pulled the trigger.

He lay on the ground and screamed, partly out of fear and partly out of pure anger, for several minutes. The person who had pulled the trigger never showed himself. He never even checked to see if Arlon was seriously injured.

By a weird but thankful quirk of fate, Arlon wasn't hurt or killed. The top of his camouflaged hat was literally blown open. An old stump a few feet to his right had saved him. It had taken the brunt of the load and was ravaged with shot.

A knot still settles in my stomach when I realize that had that stump not been there, or had Arlon been sitting even an inch or two more erect, I would have lost a good friend.

I wish I could say that Arlon is the only one of my friends who has been through such an ordeal, but he's not. Some haven't shared his "luck." What a shame that people are getting shot while doing something that should be so safe.

And I'll never understand it. I've seen thousands of turkeys and thousands of men, and I've never seen a man that looked like a turkey. There's no excuse for confusing the two, especially in the spring when the hunter should see a visible beard before firing.

But unfortunately there are some who lose sight of what turkey hunting is about. To them they *have* to kill a turkey at all costs. They see it almost as a rite of manhood and a quick and easy way to be a hero. In a sporting goods store the night before a new season I've seen the gleam in someone's eye and heard the fever in his voice as he buys a new Magnum shotgun and talks about "blowing one away."

Imagine how such a person is going to hunt. He wants a turkey so badly that every sound he hears will be interpreted as the gobbler of his dreams. He wants a turkey so badly that in his mind he sees a bird when he pulls the trigger on another human.

And what's to be done? Some have called for mandatory fluorescent orange clothing. But to me that's attacking the problem from the wrong side. The answer lies in education. Most game departments go to great lengths to teach the ways of safe turkey hunting. But safe turkey hunting rests in the hands of each individual who participates in the sport.

Don't ever think it can't happen to you, that you can't get shot or shoot someone. Take no chances.

Done correctly, turkey hunting is a sport in which the hunter sits and the bird comes to him. With that in mind, neither I nor my clients or friends ever load our guns until we're set up and calling. Your chances of walking up on a gobbler and getting a shot are slim to none anyway.

Your odds are the same for stalking within range of what might be a calling turkey. Never, never try to sneak in on hen yelps. First of all, you're after bearded gobblers, and even if the hen does have a tom with her, you'll probably never get close enough for a shot. And if those calls are coming from a hunter you could get shot . . . or worse.

Whenever you even think you hear another hunter working a bird, stay completely out of the area. No wild turkey is worth taking a chance with your life.

Yelping on a call while walking through the woods can be another disaster waiting to happen. Countless times every year, some guy with a

There is no way that a turkey hunter looks like a wild turkey gobbler, yet every year turkey hunters are mistaken for game and injured or killed. *Never* **shoot at sound or movement; always make positive identification and see a visible beard.** *Photo by Ray Eye.*

gun and a license hears some turkey calls coming down a trail. His adrenaline takes the place of caution, he sees movement, and—bang!

Now you realize why many experienced turkey hunters wear fluorescent orange when moving through the woods. When calling, they place the fluorescent orange behind their calling tree to warn hunters coming from the rear.

Don't call until you're fully set up. It's also a good idea to sit still and spend a few minutes listening and looking for signs of other hunters. Make sure you're fully camouflaged: the harder it is to see you, the harder it will be for someone to shoot you. Be sure you're not wearing any visible white, red, blue, or black which could be confused with the color of a gobbler.

As you sit, interpret each sound as that of an approaching hunter. Move only your eyes as you scan the woods. Even when you have a bird gobbling and coming and you know he's close, make sure it's not a man before you raise your gun. Several times I've had hunters suddenly materialize to replace what was supposed to be a gobbler.

Pray that it never happens, but there may come a day when you're set up and you look out and see him — a hunter heading your way. He may have stumbled on you quite by accident or he may be coming to your calls. If the latter is the case, he may be stalking you, moving slowly with his gun ready and his finger on the trigger.

I've been there and it's scary as hell. All thoughts of turkeys instantly vanish and your body shakes from head to toe. What you do next is one of the most important moves of your life.

Whatever you do, don't make any more turkey sounds. Don't draw any subtle attention to yourself: no whistling, no raised hands, . . . no movement of any kind.

Figure out a way to let him know there's a person in the area. Don't yell "hey" or some profanity. (Not yet, anyway.) Loudly say something unmistakably human, such as "Good Morning!" or "Nice day, isn't it."

Even after you've spoken out loud, don't take anything for granted. Hold perfectly still until you're absolutely sure the guy knows you're a person. Even if it's someone trespassing on your private honey hole, keep calm and take your time. Only when you see that the "hunter" is relaxed and has his gun down do you show yourself.

People have also been shot while carrying a bird through the woods. After you shoot a turkey, either wrap it in an orange vest or put it in one of the specially designed carrying bags that are on the market.

But there are reasons for accidents other than being mistaken for game. Pure carelessness could have cost me a leg when I stupidly let an excited young client crawl behind me with a loaded gun. The Magnum load of fours plowed a yard-long furrow not four inches from my legs.

I hope I haven't scared anyone away from turkey hunting. The sloppy hunters that shoot other hunters are really a very small minority. Chances are, you'll hunt all your life with no problems.

But please be aware that accidents can happen to ordinary people like you. Ask my friend Arlon. He'll tell you that accidents can happen. And unfortunately there were others who can no longer tell you. After the next season there will probably be even more.

Be careful and hunt defensively.

25

Turkeys I've Known

Eugene

I first met Eugene early in the spring of 1983, during a pre-season scouting trip to the hills where I was raised. I'd been walking the maze of old logging roads that laced the hardwoods, stopping occasionally to hoot or maybe hen call to pinpoint gobblers.

But the gobble that came from that long, high glade was like no other. It was . . . well, powerful. When that bird opened up every other turkey within hearing distance grew silent. When I came back to scout the next time, and the next, and the next, that bird was always on the same glade. His loud, rattling gobble had begun to get a hold on me.

I named him Eugene after a fat, smart-mouthed kid I knew in grade school who wouldn't utter a peep when he was close to you. But let him get across the playground where you couldn't get to him and he'd call you every name in the book.

Eugene the turkey was the same way.

He'd stand out near the lip of that glade where he could see for dozens of miles and gobble and gobble at every hoot, crow call, and hen call—as long as I kept my distance. But when I sneaked to the back side of the glade to call, he wouldn't so much as cluck. You'd swear he had disappeared.

Yet when I got to where I could view the glade, I'd see him standing there, as big as a potbellied stove. He'd stare me in the eye for a few seconds before sailing off into the valley.

He became an obsession with me. I didn't really want to kill him as much as I wanted to fool him. I studied him every chance I got, and a couple of times before the season I called him within good camera range.

This gobbler was big, probably bigger than any turkey I've ever seen. It was obvious he'd been in these hills for years. I have one slide of him strutting away from the camera that shows a pair of spurs as long and as thick as flint arrowheads.

I'll never know if Eugene was just plain smart or just plain lucky, but something kept him out of shotgun range.

The first day I was really able to work Eugene during the season, I had a partner with me, a gentleman with failing health. A 200-yard walk from the truck was for him a major hike. By the time I got the big gobbler fired up my hunter was totally exhausted.

We did our best to set up in a small tangle of limbs and vines, the only available cover. The woods were open that year and Eugene got suspicious the minute he stepped onto the opposite end of the flat. He ended up circling to the other side of the hollow and staring straight across at us. I swear he was enjoying it.

A few days later, Max Shekelton and I set out at midmorning to give Eugene a try. He was on his glade as usual, but today he had some hens and another gobbler fairly close by.

We set up and Eugene gobbled at everything, as did the other gobbler. The two toms were soon so fired up that Max and I could hear the excited purrs, pops, and thumps of a full-scale gobbler fight.

One of the turkeys finally flew off and the winner let out a victorious gobble — it was Eugene. I hit him with everything I knew, even trying to get his hens fired up, but nothing worked.

Max and I decided to go after the gobbler that had just left. It took some doing, but he finally came in and Max got him. It was tough to believe that the bird had come out second best.

Max's gobbler weighed 23½ pounds, had a 12-inch beard and spurs that were exactly 1½ inches long. But he had been beaten bad. His plumage was raked and his breast was scarred with deep gouges from Eugene's spurs.

I took a couple of clients back after Eugene a couple of days later. He wouldn't come in to calls, but I could get him to follow me as I backed out. One hunter passed up a shot he thought was too far. Afterwards we stepped off the distance and found it a little over thirty yards. Eugene had lucked out again.

That same morning I tried to pull another fast one on Eugene. Since he was starting to walk away gobbling whenever I moved in, I decided to circle him and push him toward my hunters.

I cut my circle and hooted once to find the bird's location. He gobbled from not thirty yards away, stepped into the logging road strutting, and then flew off.

The last day of the season was greeted by a gully-washing rain that flooded many roads. But my brother Marty and I took Verle Pemberton and Jim Toby, a pair of very good hunters, into the woods after Eugene. We worked in and around Eugene's glade most of the morning.

Marty finally got a trio of gobblers calling and coming in. He could tell by the gobbles that Eugene wasn't among them, but any gobbler's a good gobbler when there's only an hour left in the season.

The three toms came up and Jim Toby dropped the lead bird of twenty-one pounds. Just a split second before Jim pulled the trigger, Marty noticed movement to his right. It was Eugene, easily towering a foot above the other turkeys. Marty swung his gun but Eugene ducked, ran, and flew off into the rain.

That was the last time we saw him. He wasn't there the next spring. And for some reason, turkey hunting in those hills hasn't been the same since.

The Tombigbee Gobbler

There are times when a turkey hunter has no choice but to buck the odds and try to accomplish what is widely known as the improbable, if not the impossible. I've always held to the theory that a hunter should go for it when he has nothing to lose. He who does is often surprised at what a gobbler might do when he really wants to.

Ben Held and I had gone to Alabama for some seminars and calling contests, but more importantly for some turkey hunting. I've always rated the easterns of Alabama as some of the toughest turkeys in America. Even though there are lots of them, getting one in front of a gun is a challenge for the best of hunters.

That particular day the challenge seemed especially tough.

Ben and I were the guests of David Crowe and his brother, Bob. We were hunting a good-looking stretch of woods and fields that bordered the Tombigbee River. The problem was that the habitat was equally good on the other side of the river, and that was where the turkeys were.

We fanned out and hunted our side of the river hard, but by mid-morning all that was left to do was call to turkeys across the river. I had one bird on the other side eating out of my hand; he was gobbling at everything. But prospects didn't look good with two hundred yards of water between us.

As I lay there in the grass, I thought back to all the times I'd seen gobblers flying across rivers in the Ozarks. Though the Ozark rivers were small compared to the Tombigbee, I'd seen a lot of turkeys sail across them as if it was an everyday event. Surely these Alabama birds did the same thing. After all, our side of the river had been full of turkeys the day before and I doubted that they'd put on swim fins or chartered a ferry.

Comparing mental notes on all of the birds I'd seen back home, I realized that turkeys seemed to cross at favored places. Maybe these Alabama birds did the same. I grabbed my gear and went on a quick scouting mission.

Sure enough, I found a small sandbar downstream that melted into open woods. It was absolutely covered with turkey tracks. At first I thought this might be a place where the birds went to water. Checking closer, I saw several big gobbler tracks that simply disappeared at the water's edge.

I backed up into the nearby trees and started calling. The bird I'd worked earlier was still fired up. I could hear the bird getting closer and closer to the river's far bank. Finally I could see him strutting back and forth on a small sandbar across from me.

Figuring I had nothing to lose I poured the calls to him. I admit to being more than a little surprised when he dropped out of strut, took a few steps, and sailed across the river toward me.

The turkey landed amid the tracks on the sandbar in front of me, gobbled, and went into strut. I called and he folded up and headed my way.

To this day I don't know what I did, but somehow I spooked that bird and he headed back toward the river. I tried a shot with the muzzleloader I was carrying but hit only the air where the turkey had been.

David Crowe had been close enough to hear the whole thing. We agreed it was a special accomplishment to have gotten the bird across the water; it would have been just a little nicer if I'd had the bird to show for it.

We were back on the same property the next morning. Aside from a gobbler that we spooked off his roost, all of the birds still seemed to be on the other side of the river.

Figuring I still had nothing to lose, I headed to the place where I'd missed the chance of a lifetime the day before. This time I decided to set up closer to the sandbar. As for calls, I used old reliable — my voice.

A gobble sounded from the place where I'd started the bird the day before. I increased my intensity and the bird responded some more. To make a long story short, I ended up calling nearly nonstop for close to forty-five minutes. The bird came to within three hundred yards of the river's edge, where he strutted back and forth, gobbling with almost every breath. Growing hoarse, I sent one last series of excited cutting across to the bird.

The gobbler flapped his wings and went into a glide that brought him to the same spot on the sandbar he'd flown to yesterday. He shook himself off and stepped up onto the river bank. I got it right the second time.

David Crowe was on the scene in seconds. He'd been set up where he could see the whole thing.

We'll never know for sure if that was the same longbeard I'd called across and missed the day before. But the bird had responded the same, had come from the same spot, and had even looked the same.

The Confused Merriam

Just when you think you're really starting to understand turkeys, you happen across one that leaves you totally dumbfounded. I'm not talking about birds that are super shy and seemingly impossible to call. I'm talking about turkeys that seem, well, . . . crazy.

I met such a bird the first day I ever hunted the Merriams of South Dakota's Black Hills. It was an afternoon hunt and I was guiding a gentleman from Minnesota for John Hauer. A third hunter tagged along.

John dropped us off in some of the prettiest turkey country I'd ever seen. Rolling hills of ponderosa pines lay separated by small meadows. A gin-clear little stream bisected the property.

The shadows were stretching far across the meadow when I got a bird to gobble at my version of an elk bugle that I made with a triple-reed diaphragm. We hurried across a big open field and over a fence as we tried to get to the bird before he flew up to roost.

I made some hen calls at the edge of the timber where the bird had gobbled. Nothing. I tried again. Still nothing. I tried another elk bugle and a bird gobbled, but the sound came from the area we'd just left. "We might as well go roost him for the morning," I told the client.

As we stepped out of the timber I looked up and there, not thirty steps from where I'd bugled the first time, was a turkey. Even at close to 350 yards you could tell it was a big old gobbler in strut. I made some loud hen calls but the bird showed no response.

Since this was the client's first turkey hunt I decided to bugle again so that the client could use his binoculars to watch a turkey gobble. I bugled, the bird gobbled, and then he took off on a dead run—right at us!

I hen called again and the bird slowed to a walk. When I followed with a bugle, he gobbled and came at us full speed.

There we were, three of us standing in the open, with basically nothing but three hundred yards of open field between us and a kamikaze turkey. When the gobbler dropped from sight in a slight gully, the three of us hurried to a scraggly stand of trees fifty yards away.

The gobbler had slowed a bit when he came back into view. Trying to hurry him along, I hit him with aggressive hen calls and he slowed even more. "Bugle again," somebody said. I did, and the bird gobbled hard and broke into a sprint, coming right at us. I never hen called to that Merriam again.

"This isn't exactly your normal turkey hunt," I told the novice from Minnesota. There we were, sitting in the middle of a few spindly pines surrounded by nothing but grass and wildflowers, being charged by some elk-hating turkey. To top it off, it was nearly too dark to shoot.

The bird continued at us on a dead run, his long beard swinging like a pendulum back and forth in front of his chest. Things looked good; the client had his gun up and was holding as steady as a rock.

But when the gobbler was seventy yards out he saw the third member of our party. Still the turkey kept coming, now angling a little to our right but still approaching on a dead run. Nothing I could do would stop him.

When he passed by, we took our best shot. Unscathed, the gobbler never broke stride or showed any alarm. He continued on across the meadow and disappeared into the pines behind us.

It just goes to show: there's no figuring turkeys.

26

Turkey Tales

Francis

Most of the hunters a person meets while guiding are fine people. Over the years I've been fortunate to have guided people from all walks of life. Many have become cherished friends.

But every once in a while I get someone like Francis. Francis had booked a spring hunt and showed a lot of enthusiasm, calling me weekly to make sure the hunt was on. He showed up a half-hour early the morning of the hunt.

You could tell by his lily-white skin and brand new hunting clothes that Francis was something of a stranger to the outdoors. But he was exceptionally pleasant and eager. We loaded up my jeep and took off.

When we got atop the ridge I wanted to hunt, Francis pulled a shiny Remington 1100 out of a case. I mean you could tell by the looks and smell of the gun that it was fresh out of the box and unfired. Next he reached for a box of three-inch Magnum shells, wrapping his manicured fingers around the first layer of the box.

The next time I looked, there was Francis, shells in one hand, shotgun in the other, and a very puzzled look on his face as he glanced from one to the other. "Excuse me," he finally said, "could you please tell me where the bullets go?"

"Sure," I replied. Opening a pocket on my coat, I said, "How about the bullets go right here until we need them."

It was the kind of morning guides usually see only in their dreams. The birds gobbled hard on the roost and didn't quiet throughout the morning.

Francis and I started the morning setting up about 150 yards from a gobbler that was sounding off like a broken record. I gave the bird a few soft yelps. He flew down and hit the ground gobbling.

It was about then that the gobbler and a smaller tom walked into view. "Hey, it looks like there's two of them," Francis said loudly, obviously proud that he could see them.

Being a little loud was a problem that would plague Francis throughout the day. He traversed the Ozark hills with all the finesse of a man dragging a ball and chain—on each foot. Each time we'd begin to move in on a bird, he'd spook it.

Then I came up with a scheme I thought would surely work. At the head of a hollow I stopped, turned to Francis, and whispered, "We have to really be quiet when we're walking through this area . . . ridgegators."

"Ridgegators?" Francis questioned. "Yeah," I said, "they're kind of like alligators with hooved feet and they live up in these hills. They're real tough to see because they have a dead-leaf pattern on their backs. They just hold real still and when they hear a mouse or squirrel running through the leaves they snap out and grab it."

"Really?" Francis asked. "Yeah, but sometimes they'll snap at anything rustling in the leaves," I continued. "I had a client making too much noise up here last week and SNAP! It looked like he'd sat on an open blender."

My plan worked. Francis moved through the woods as quiet as a feather in the wind.

We were sneaking down an old logging trail when a gobbler answered one of my hoots. The bird was close enough that I could hear the rattle in his gobble, and I guessed he was just off the lip of the ridge maybe sixty yards away.

I whispered for Francis to sneak up to an old oak in front of me, handed him a "bullet," and told him to shoot the bird in the face as soon as he saw a beard.

Francis sneaked to the oak without so much as rustling a leaf. When he was all set, he carefully placed the shell in the gun's chamber. Then with a single finger he pushed the little silver button that forced the action home with a crash that echoed down the hollow.

Looking over the top of his pop-bottle-thick glasses Francis turned to me and whispered, "O.K., Ray, call that S.O.B. up." We hunted the rest of the morning but couldn't get Francis a shot at a bird.

After we left the woods we stopped at a little country tavern for a cheeseburger and beer and to see how other hunters had fared. The place got kind of quiet when my obviously misplaced friend and I walked up to the bar and straddled a couple of stools.

Things eventually picked back up in the bar. People started talking, and the sounds of turkey calls floated throughout. You could see Francis starting to feel more at ease. Finally, doing his best to fit in, Francis turned to the old stubble-faced backwoodsman sitting beside him, slid the hat back on his balding head and said, "Boy, the damn ridgegators are really bad this year, ain't they?"

The Cow and the Gobbler

Down in southern Missouri there used to be an old gobbler that roosted up on a ridge where a farmer, a half-crazy old bachelor, swore he'd shoot anybody caught hunting on his place.

Every morning the gobbler would sail off the roost and land in the middle of a huge pasture, calling to hens as he stood out there and strutted among the Herefords. The owner of the pasture let most of the locals hunt, and almost everybody had given the tom a try.

Hunters would set up on the edge of the pasture and try to call, but the bird wouldn't ever budge. People tried decoys, hen calling, gobbling, and jake yelping, but nothing made any difference: the gobbler wouldn't move.

Hunters even tried sneaking to the field's edge, hoping to get a shot at the gobbler as he left the field, but the bird always managed to fly from the center of the field untouched.

Every day of the season someone would stop at the local café with a tale of frustration at trying to kill that turkey. Finally a couple of hunters in our camp, Mark and H.D., came up with what they said would be a sure-fire — and legal — way to kill that old gobbler. Bets and wagers started flying, with all the locals swearing that old tom just couldn't be killed.

That night I pulled Mark aside and asked him about his plan. Heck, I may not be the best turkey hunter in the world but I've called in more than my share of turkeys and I knew that bird had made a fool out of me and everyone in the county who owned a turkey call.

Mark explained that he and H.D. had made themselves a red and white cow suit. They knew that the gobbler wasn't spooked by cows, and they figured they'd just ease out into the field and put the hurt on him.

Mark and H.D. were at the edge of the cow pasture long before dawn the next morning with the cow suit in two pieces. Mark was to take the front piece while H.D. brought up the rear. When they got close enough to the gobbler they'd slide a shotgun out the peephole Mark was using, and the gobbler, as well as the bets, would be theirs.

Sure enough, at first light the gobbler gobbled a couple of times on the roost and sailed down to the middle of the pasture. Mark and H.D. started easing out into the field, H.D. holding the stock of the shotgun while Mark held the barrel and acted as the cow's eyes.

All bent over and unable to see, H.D. kept asking Mark about their position. "Where's he at?" H.D. asked. "He's still about seventy yards out," Mark whispered. "I don't want to head right at him. Let's just take our time and get closer."

They moved real slowly and easily; first Mark took a step and then H.D. took a step to catch up. Another ten minutes passed and H.D. said, "How we doing? Let's hurry and make him a jellyhead so I can get out of this suit and straighten up."

"Just be patient," said Mark. "He's about forty-five yards out and I think it's going to work. He's totally ignoring us. Just fifteen more yards and we'll smoke him."

The cloth cow steadily inched across the pasture. Suddenly Mark stopped in his tracks and H.D. slammed into his back. "Why'd you stop?" H.D. asked.

"There's a bull looking at us," said Mark. "Don't worry about that damn bull," H.D. said. "I don't care about any old bull. Keep moving so we can double-team that turkey."

Mark started off again but stopped when they were just out of gun range. H.D. slammed into his back again. "What's wrong this time?" H.D. asked.

"Uh-oh, that bull I told you about, he's hurrying this way with a strange look in his eye," said Mark.

"What are we going to do?" H.D. asked.

"Well, I'm going to act like I'm eating some grass," said Mark. "But partner, you'd better brace yourself."

Store-bought Yelper

Being the kind of kid I was, the kind that drove my family crazy with nonstop talk of turkey hunting, I somehow got passed off onto Uncle Lee. The patient soul he was, good old Uncle Lee always had time to talk hunting with me and to make sure I got out during the season. He also introduced me to some of the most colorful characters I've ever met.

Old Joe was one of Lee's closest hunting buddies. About as Ozark as you could get, Joe always wore a brown toothy smile across a face that was usually covered with a tobacco-stained stubbly beard. No one knew for sure if old Joe either didn't know how to tie his boots or was just too lazy to do so. He did manage to zipper his pants about half of the time, though.

One afternoon Uncle Lee and I were in his yard when Joe's '53 Chevrolet pickup truck came barreling onto the property. You could see Joe's ear-to-ear smile despite the cobwebs of cracks that covered his windshield.

He got out of his truck and proudly boasted that he had a brand new, store-bought mouth yelper. Now we'd seen mouth calls before, but they'd always been made of plumber's lead and a condom from the men's room down at the gas station.

"Looky here," said Joe. "I'm gonna be the very first turkey hunter in Iron County to kill hisself a turkey with a fancy store-bought mouth call."

"Well, what's it sound like?" asked Uncle Lee.

"I ain't opened it yet but it'll sound real good," said Joe. "It says right here on the back all you do is put it in your mouth, put your tongue on the call, blow air, and it's guaranteed to make all the calls of the wild turkey."

"I don't know," said Uncle Lee. "I think you might want to do some practicing on it." Joe just scoffed at the idea and shoved the package into his pocket.

Joe's old Chevy rolled into Lee's driveway about four the next morning, the opening day of turkey season. We could see Joe inside his cab, using a cigarette lighter to read and re-read the instructions for the call, which was still in its package.

We drove up an old logging road to the top of the mountain behind my grandma's house. When Uncle Lee and I left Joe, he was walking out onto an open glade and just getting out his knife to take the mouth yelper out of its wrapping.

Uncle Lee and I headed down the ridge just as it began to get light. The songbirds were starting to sing and the whole woods was beginning to wake up as a light orange color spread across the east.

At about that time we heard a great horned owl hoot in the distance. Then a turkey gobbled. Shortly thereafter, another turkey gobbled down near the place where we'd last seen Joe.

And then we heard it. A low, grunting kind of gagging cough came from the same general area. "What was that, Uncle Lee?" I asked. "I'm not exactly sure," answered Lee.

Lee waited a few moments, then hooted like a barred owl, and a turkey gobbled just down the ridge. Then we heard that terrible gagging sound again, only this time it was louder and deeper. "I sure hope that's not Joe dying," said Uncle Lee. "We'd better go check."

When we got to him, Joe was sprawled out on his hands and knees. Sweat was pouring from his pale white face and he was gasping for air.

Uncle Lee put his hand on Joe's shoulder and said, "My God, Joe, are you all right? I tried to tell you that you should've tried using that thing before we got into the woods. Look at you, it's gobbling time! Are you going to make it?"

Joe looked up, tears running down his cheeks, and said, "I, I, I think I swallered it."

"Swallowed it, are you sure?" asked Uncle Lee.

"I think so," said Joe. "I've been through three piles of puke and haven't found it yet."

27

The Future

Most sportsmen would agree that there's something special about turkey hunting. It's the kind of sport that, once tried, is seldom abandoned.

But turkey hunting can't continue totally on its own. Just as the sport needed help a half century ago getting to where it is now, modern turkey hunting is going to need help in the next fifty years as well.

It seems like every year we see more and more factors that work toward taking the sport we consider so important away from us. Such things as loss of habitat and groups supporting unrealistic concepts of animal rights and gun laws are very real threats to absolutely every sportsman.

We encourage—no, we outright ask—that all hunters join such organizations as the National Wild Turkey Federation and other pro-hunting associations. It's important that sportsmen not only join, but that they get involved as well, donating both time and money.

We can't survive by just complaining among ourselves. Hunters need to take an active stand, writing letters to politicians and government agencies. Just as importantly, we need to police our own ranks, working on hunter safety, education, and landowner-sportsman relations.

We almost lost turkey hunting once, but we were lucky enough to get it back through a lot of hard work. The next time we lose it we probably won't get another chance.

We hope you'll help preserve what we so enjoy for the future.

Good, safe hunting.